THE
80 MINUTE MBA

Everything You'll Never Learn at Business School

Richard Reeves
and
John Knell

headline

First published in Great Britain in 2009 by
HEADLINE PUBLISHING GROUP

First published in paperback in 2014 by
HEADLINE PUBLISHING GROUP

1

Cataloguing in Publication Data is available from the British Library

ISBN 978 1 4722 2362 3

Offset in ITC Century by Avon DataSet Ltd,
Bidford-on-Avon, Warwickshire

Printed and bound by CPI Group (UK) Ltd, Croydon, CR0 4YY

Headline's policy is to use papers that are natural, renewable and
recyclable products and made from wood grown in sustainable forests.
The logging and manufacturing processes are expected to conform to the
environmental regulations of the country of origin.

HEADLINE PUBLISHING GROUP
An Hachette UK Company
338 Euston Road
London NW1 3BH

www.headline.co.uk
www.hachette.co.uk

DEDICATION

This book is dedicated to all those who refuse
to see business education as an oxymoron.

ACKNOWLEDGEMENTS

We'd like to thank the man who helped us put *The 80 Minute MBA* into the market, Brendan Barnes, from the London Business Forum. Richard Jolly of London Business School for his wisdom and expertise. Matthew Gwyther and Andrew Saunders from *Management Today* who allowed Richard to opine on many of these issues for several years; and the numerous clients with whom we have worked, and from whom we have learned so much. Last but not least, John Moseley from Headline, who has perfectly maintained the delicate balance of patience and pressure required to bring this project to its conclusion.

CONTENTS

CITIUS EST MELIUS

(Quicker is better)

INTRODUCTION

You're busy, we know. Too busy to read many of the thousands of business books published each year. Perhaps too busy to attend very many 'professional development' courses. And certainly too pressed to take a year or two out to do an MBA course. You may in any case be sceptical of how much you can really learn from the gurus, professors and corporate titans who line up to proffer their advice.

We're with you. Business courses and books can, of course, be enlightening and inspiring. But more often they are a mixture of the blindingly obvious and wildly utopian. In the years we've been researching and advising on organisational issues, we've realised the value of simply cutting to the chase. No throat-clearing, winding anecdotes or lengthy case studies: just the key insights and killer facts.

This book contains the distillate of an MBA course. Just as the creators of the Reduced Shakespeare Company brought the works of the Bard to the stage in shortened format, so we have attempted to bring the best of business thinking into a single, slim volume, drawing on a presentation of the same name which we have been delivering over the last year or so. *The 80 Minute MBA* should do what it says on the tin. So if you read slightly quicker than the average person (and we know you do) this book should only take an hour and twenty minutes to read. Like all self-respecting MBA courses, ours has a motto: *citius est melius* – quicker is better.

We've had a good time synthesising the material – remembering Noël Coward reckoned that work was 'more fun than fun' – and hope that comes across in what follows. But we are deadly serious about the potential of organisations and their leaders to create better work, more economic value and stronger human relationships. We can be sceptical, but we hope never cynical. An irreducible core of optimism runs through our work. Business life can be – should be – good.

But it is also clear that we are writing against darkening skies. In the first half of 2008, the scientific evidence that global heating is reaching a dangerous tipping point – beyond which any action will be at best remedial – became incontrovertible. In the second half of 2008, the world's financial system shattered, with the loss of mammoth players such as Lehman's, trillions of dollars of taxpayers' money and all confidence in the capital markets. The political economy of the West has been profoundly reshaped. Our MBA is one constructed in clear sight of a broken planet and a broken financial system.

We are not dismissive of MBAs: the best provide inspiring teachers, opportunities for intellectual interrogation, a challenging peer group and space for reflection. On the other hand, they can be personally enervating. Here's a description from one slightly disenchanted graduate: 'I was beginning to feel what would become a familiar set of sensations. The life-sapping effect of fluorescent lighting. The vague stench of Styrofoam and Chinese noodles drifting up from the waste basket. Dehydration and itching skin. The realization that half the people in the room were checking e-mail and surfing the web, which explained why any questions lingered in the air for seconds before stimulating an answer... Words and ideas drifted between us in slow motion. It was nearly midnight when we gave up.'[1]

But there is no doubt that the ethos of some MBA programmes is part of the problem rather than the solution. The high-octane, risk-taking, money-chasing approach favoured by some graduates may have contributed to the overreach of many firms in the run up to 2008. There is some evidence that business school students become less ethical in their outlook and behaviour during the course of their studies.[2] Graduates of business school are more likely than their non-business peers to cheat.[3] Education corrupts; business education corrupts absolutely.

The post-2008 world requires a new spirit of stewardship in business leaders, a new focus on building businesses that are both environmentally and financially sustainable. We focus a good deal of our limited time on sustainability: for this we make no apology. Our planet is broken, and organisations have a responsibility to help fix it. But it is equally important that businesses are economically sustainable too – resting on secure financial foundations, emphasising organic growth rather than debt-fuelled mergers and acquisitions activity, and rewarding executives for their performance over a period of years, rather than months. The broken financial system[4] needs a new approach, a new moral philosophy of business.

There are some things, though, that do not change. One is that no self-respecting business book is complete without a model or diagram. And we're not quite brave enough to do without one. So here's ours,

The 80 Minute MBA 'tornado':

At the very top, as you now probably expect, is **Sustainability**. This book is about success: as a leader, a manager and in organisational terms. But ensuring the future of our fragile, threatened planet must now run through everything we do. The next tornado ring is **Leadership** – a core component of any MBA programme. Then it's the three Cs: culture, cash and conversation. **Culture** – what brings organisations together, why do people matter, how do we engage them? **Cash** – covering finance, balance sheets, accounting, supply chain management and economics. **Conversation** – how do you talk to your markets and your customers? Along the way there are also mini-modules on strategy, ethics, time management, economics, statistics and neuromarketing.

We realise that for some of you even 80 minutes may sound like a big chunk of time to carve out of your hectic schedules. Again, we sympathise: we've had some requests for the '60 Minute MBA', and for the 'half-hour version'. All we can promise is that we'll keep working on it. So, for those of you with no intention of reading any further, our thanks for your time. You've clearly gleaned what you need. If you haven't yet bought the book and the spine is undamaged, you can probably put it carefully back on the shelf (and try to forget that between us we've got five children). If you can spare another seventy-seven minutes, however, we promise not to waste a single one.

SUSTAIN-
ABILITY

We cannot measure national spirit by the Dow Jones Average, nor national achievement by the Gross National Product. For the Gross National Product includes air pollution, and ambulances to clear our highways from carnage...The Gross National Product includes the destruction of the redwoods and the death of Lake Superior. It grows with the production of napalm and missiles and nuclear warheads... It includes the broadcasting of television programs which glorify violence to sell goods to our children.

Robert F. Kennedy, 18 March 1968

Sustainability is not a major feature on the curricula of many MBA courses. Not yet, anyway. But it is a major concern for business leaders around the world. An understanding of the challenges of sustainable living, and a commitment to act in order to meet them are now prerequisites of leadership. We broke the financial system in 2008; we've been breaking the planet for decades. Some business schools get it. David Schmittlein, Dean of MIT Sloan, says: 'It's not a story of 28-year-olds trying to save the world. It's a story of managing cataclysmic change. It's about what our students do and need to say when they get into these organisations.'

Environmental campaigners have changed their image in recent years:

Daniel Hooper, aka Swampy – the one on the left – made his name hiding in tunnels to stop road developments and appearing on various TV quiz shows. In the good old days, green activists were scruffy, young and idealistic. Now look at the new model activist on the right: Stuart Rose, Chairman of Marks and Spencer. His 'Plan A' has put the retailer in the forefront of the fight against climate change. (An ungenerous fashion critic might suggest that Swampy is also modelling M&S clothes from its most difficult years.) The 100-point Plan A will make the company carbon-neutral, reduce the proportion of its waste going into landfill to zero, switch over time to organic cotton, and move towards fairly traded products.

'We're doing this because it's what you want us to do,' said Rose. 'It's also the right thing to do. We're calling it Plan A because we believe it's now the only way to do business. There is no Plan B.' Even as the economic climate puts pressure on the retailer, the commitment to sustainability appears to be holding, and M&S's competitors are trying hard to catch up. In the US, Wal-Mart is moving quickly to reduce waste and unnecessary energy loss. Such is the power of the retail giant that a recent decision to stock only concentrated laundry detergent will save annually 400 million gallons of water, 95 million pounds of plastic resin and 125 million pounds of cardboard, as well as the energy required to manufacture and ship all this excess packaging.

'Climate change is not an issue that can be solved in competition among businesses,' says Ben Verwaayen, CEO of British Telecom Group. 'It must be the number one priority for both governments and the business community.' Richard Branson, Chairman of Virgin, believes, 'We must rapidly wean ourselves off our dependence on coal and fossil fuels.' Wal-Mart's CEO, Lee Scott, claims that sustainability is 'the single biggest business opportunity of the twenty-first century'. Nicholas Stern, the hard-headed economist commissioned by the UK government to examine climate change, warned of the 'greatest and widest-ranging market failure ever seen' if companies fail to become sustainable.[1]

What's changed? Why are sustainability issues moving from the business margins to the mainstream? The short answer is: the facts. The sheer weight of evidence showing that the combined effects of

'We're running an uncontrolled experiment on the only home we have.'
Bill Collins, Berkeley National Laboratory, California

population growth, climate change and scarcity of land, water, energy and food are highly likely to destabilise global society, spark conflict and result in the death of millions of people. The best business leaders are following the lead of the economist John Maynard Keynes, who famously declared, 'When the facts change, I change my mind. What do you do, Sir?'

THE FACTS

Sustainability is about living within ecological means. The most famous definition of sustainable development was given in the Brundtland Report of 1987: 'Meeting the needs of the present generation without compromising the ability of future generations to meet their needs.'

Climate change is, of course, the central sustainability issue right now – and is our principal focus in this chapter. But the related issues of population growth and resource scarcity fall under the sustainability imperative too. The world's population is forecast to rise from 6.7 billion to 9.2 billion between now and 2050: the increase of 2.5 billion is greater than the total global population in 1950. Most of the usable land in Asia is already under cultivation, which is why the Chinese government is buying land in the Philippines, Uganda, Australia and Mexico. As oil supplies run low, the price of petrochemical fertilisers will rise, making food more expensive: the 2007 price spikes reduced cultivation of Kenya's Rift Valley by a third, according to the BBC.

The 'big one', however, is global warming. The world's climate is being heated by our activities, in a way that threatens our own prospects as well as those of other species. So far our response has been lacklustre at best. It is mass, slow suicide. Thomas L. Friedman, in his book *Hot, Flat and Crowded*, puts it like this: 'Human society has been like the proverbial frogs in the pail on the stove, where the heat gets turned up very slightly every hour, so the frog never thinks to jump out. It just keeps adjusting until it boils to death.' The irony, of course, is that we are turning up the heat on ourselves.

The dwindling, eccentric band of climate change deniers will sometimes point out that levels of carbon dioxide and other gases heating the globe have fluctuated over time. True enough. But you don't have to be a climatologist to look at the following graph – which takes a 2,000-year time frame – to reckon there is something different about recent years. Global average temperature, sea level and northern hemisphere snow cover all tell the same story. The Intergovernmental Panel on Climate Change reported that sea levels are rising at 20 times the average rate over the last 3,000 years (see graphs opposite).

Admittedly, there is huge uncertainty about how quickly the rise in global temperatures will hit weather systems, water levels and crop yields – and the scale of the changes. But the risk is that it will be much worse than we think. The atmosphere is heating up towards a potentially catastrophic 'tipping point'. If you ask experts in the field about their biggest worry, frequently the single-word answer is: ice. The reduction of the polar ice is a big worry, because the white caps act as a coolant system, reflecting back the sun's rays. In the summer of 2007 the area covered by Arctic ice shrank to 1.6 million square miles. The ice always contracts over the summer, but not this much: the previous low was 2.05 million square miles, recorded just two years earlier.

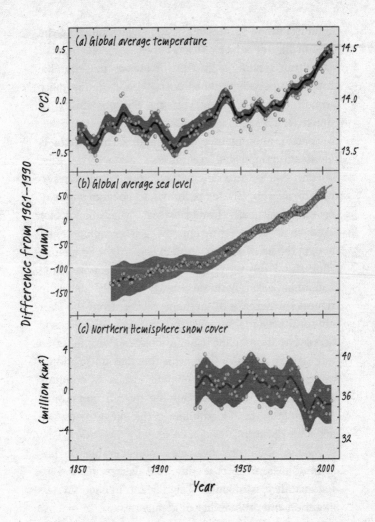

(a) Global average temperature

(b) Global average sea level

(c) Northern Hemisphere snow cover

Difference from 1961–1990

Year

But melting ice also threatens to cause a bigger, more sudden shock to the planet's system, in one of two ways. First, there is a growing danger that a big chunk of ice will slide into the sea, as meltwater loosens the underbelly of the huge ice sheets of Greenland and Antarctica. The Larsen B shelf cracked in 1987. Fifteen years later, 1,300 square miles of the shelf broke off into giant ice cubes, some the size of Manhattan. There is growing evidence that the ice sheets are becoming more unstable and sliding more quickly into the ocean, raising the possibility of catastrophic rises in sea level.[2]

Second, the melting of permafrost in Siberia is releasing dangerous greenhouse gases. The East Siberian Sea is 'bubbling with methane' according to recent research.[3] There are known to be large stores of the gas underneath the permafrost, which has so far acted as a 'lid' to prevent the gas escaping. Now, though, the lid is leaking. Project leader Igor Semiletov, from the University of Alaska, told reporters in December 2008: 'With this newly obtained data, we suggest an increase of methane release from the East Siberian Arctic shelf. We have obtained a drastic increase of air methane in some sites – sometimes up to four times higher than the background [global average].' The science of climate change is complex and constantly changing. But the overall message is clear. Unless we decarbonise economic growth, we face a bleak future.

As the data has become unanswerable, it has become clearer by the day that issues related to sustainability will have a significant impact on the operation and profitability of businesses.

THE BUSINESS IMPACT

Eight of ten FTSE500 companies consider climate change to present a 'commercial risk' – but the same proportion regard it as a 'commercial opportunity for both existing and new products'.[4] They are right on both counts, but the opportunities have yet to be seized. Climate change poses three kinds of business risk:

- PHYSICAL RISKS, INCLUDING RISING SEA LEVELS, EXTREME WEATHER AND CROP FAILURES
- REGULATORY RISKS, E.G. EMISSIONS CURBS AND TOUGHER ENVIRONMENTAL TAX SCHEMES
- REPUTATIONAL RISKS, AS CUSTOMERS, EMPLOYEES AND INVESTORS GO GREEN

PHYSICAL RISKS – DROWNING, NOT WAVING

Who cares about rising sea levels or changing crop patterns? Well, you care if you live on a low-lying island. At the end of 2008, the government of the Maldives embarked on a search for a new home, in readiness to move the entire population when the islands are covered in water: a twenty-first-century Exodus. You should, then, care out of simple human decency. But even in strict business terms, you should also be concerned about the possible impact on your properties, people and supply lines.

You should, very obviously, be concerned if you own a hotel chain, or have sizeable investments in beachfront hotels in warm, sunny places. The tourist industry in general is one of the five sectors in the 'danger zone' according to a comprehensive KPMG survey. It is ill-prepared for the potentially dramatic influence of climate change. Some nations are taking notice. The Australian Business Roundtable on Climate Change points out that the country's $32 billion tourist industry is highly climate-dependent. The Great Barrier Reef supports a $1.5 billion industry, but following a 2–3°C increase in temperature, 97% of the reef could be bleached white – and who'll go snorkelling then? In the Alps, winter sport will remain viable only in areas above 1,800 metres.

The growing problems of scarcity of goods such as water, food and energy will also be exacerbated by climate change and directly hit a wide range of companies. Firms which rely on products that grow in certain threatened areas need to prepare quickly for the likely consequences of global heating: coffee companies whose beans are grown in parts of the world forecast to run out of water; beverage and beer producers who use water in their African and Indian bottling operations. This is also an area where brands are likely to come under increasing attack from campaigners. Coca-Cola has faced criticism for its use of water in its bottling plants in water-scarce areas; a plant in Plachimada, Kerala was shut down in 2004. Coca-Cola denies any wrongdoing.[5] Large organisations are having to look hard at their supply chain, to see where its points of climate-related weakness are. Hopefully, the exercise also helps to strengthen corporate resolve to mitigate these effects.

Smart investors are looking harder at climate-change effects too. Financiers, who have plenty to worry about just staying in business, are also worrying a great deal about climate change – partly because of insurance risks around this issue, but also because they want to know how much risk is in their investment portfolio. A chief executive of a major bank said to one of the authors recently, 'We need to know how much carbon is in our portfolio.' Not just risk and debt, but how much *carbon*. 'Over the past few decades, insured loss amounts as a result of natural disasters have grown several times over, from below $4 billion in 1970 to $21 billion in 1990,' warns Ivo Menzinger, Managing Director of Sustainability and Emerging Risk Management at Swiss Re, the world's largest reinsurance company. 'In 2005, losses were over $100 billion, mostly as a result of a particularly destructive hurricane season.'[6]

COUNTING THE (CARBON) COST

Governments have not acted as swiftly as necessary to reduce humanity's climate-wrecking activities. In fact, let's be clear. The paralysis of our national leaders represents the greatest political failure in human history. But there is some cause for hoping that 2009 will mark a real effort, not least because of changes in the leadership of the world's second-biggest polluter (China overtook the US in late 2008). Barack

Obama, the US President, has promised a 'new chapter' in the fight against climate change. At the end of 2008 he appointed Stephen Chu, an academic expert on renewable energy, as his Energy Secretary, and John Holdren, a leading climate-change scientist, as his Chief Scientific Advisor. So he may even have meant it. The European Union, following the UK's lead, has agreed to cut carbon emissions by 20% from their 1990 levels before 2020, and has imposed tighter emissions regulations on the car industry.

As the cost of carbon rises, the impact on your business will, of course, depend on what kind of business you're in. Take two UK plcs with a similar turnover in 2006/2007, around £12 billion: Scottish and Southern Energy and Lloyds TSB. (Of course, the bank will turn over somewhat less in 2007/08!) But if the finances look similar, the carbon output is unsurprisingly dramatically different: 26 billion tonnes of carbon dioxide from Scottish and Southern Energy, and 0.189 billion tonnes from Lloyds TSB. We know this only because they both voluntarily provide this information to the Carbon Disclosure Project: within five years you can bet (and hope) this kind of reporting will be compulsory.

These are, of course, extreme examples, from each end of the spectrum. The point is that the impact of more expensive carbon will vary by sector and firm, and that for any savvy company, the economic case for cutting emissions will become even more transparent than it is now. The highly variable carbon emissions of different firms also means it's easier for some companies to go 'carbon neutral' than it is for others. Companies with tiny carbon footprints can fairly easily claim to have gone neutral. This is not to decry those efforts – all firms should be heading this way – but it is to say that for a professional services firm, their environmental impact is much less to do with their own carbon emissions than the products and services they offer their clients and the nature of their conversations with them. What would we think of a management consultancy firm that proudly declared its carbon neutrality, while advising a client on how to get government approval for extra runways?

Of course, there is no need to wait for new laws and rules. There is a very great deal companies can do right now to make their buildings more energy-efficient, many of which would also save them money, ranging from switching to natural cooling systems and solar panels to fitting a £15 timer on a soft drinks machine to turn it off at night and weekends – which saves about £160 off the annual electricity bill. In terms of hard cash, the case for quicker action is strong. Turning lights and computers off at night – so simple a measure to implement – would save a good deal of money.

Now here's a novel idea: a computer keyboard that captures the energy from depressing the keys and uses it to help power the hard drive.

OK. It's actually an April fool's joke – which one of the authors fell for. But part of the joke – the idea of measuring your 'carbon fingerprint' – is beginning to catch on as a label for IT-related carbon emissions.

GREEN GOODNESS

If the commercial argument for greener business is good, the moral case is unanswerable. Humankind has broken the planet, but it is not – not quite – too late to fix it. So far our arguments ought to have found favour with the most hard-bitten CFO. If climate change directly threatens the bottom line, either by shattering supply chains or increasing tax bills, the case for business preparedness is clear. But in both of these cases, the business leader is responding intelligently to outside forces. The point, though, to adapt Karl Marx, should not simply be to react to the world – but to change it. Businesses have a significant responsibility for the activities damaging our world. The question is whether they are willing to bear this responsibility and do something about it. Even organisations led by people who understand the seriousness of the challenge find it difficult to make the necessary shift in culture and operations. They are victims of what psychologists call 'path dependency' – in other words, doing what they have always done. But this is now the path to mutual destruction.

Some firms are acting, but most remain trapped in old-think. They blame consumers for being unwilling to pay extra for greener products when much of the time they should be cheaper anyway because of reduced packaging and fewer resources used.[7] Or they blame governments for failing to provide a level, green playing field. Both arguments have some apparent force, but in the context of our planetary crisis they are simply pitiful. Any business that can survive only by threatening the survival of future generations through its polluting activities should not, in fact, survive. The intersection of business and the environment therefore raises profound ethical questions about the purpose and responsibility of business.

COMPLETE KANT – ETHICS IN BUSINESS

A number of MBA courses now contain modules on ethics; there are even some which specialise in corporate social responsibility. But in most cases they are not central to the agenda. The reinvention of leadership taking place in the wake of the breaking of the world's financial system will be an ethical enterprise. And a focus on sustainability is part of a new, properly ethical approach to business.

Business ethics covers matters large and small. According to a survey conducted by MORI for Management Today *and the Institute for Business Ethics in 2006, 49% of employees said it was 'acceptable' to take pens home from work, while 49% thought it was not. (For the remaining 2% this was presumably too demanding an ethical dilemma.) Of course, given the rise of flexible working, the pen may well be still being used on organisational matters – and, oh let's face it, we really don't give a monkey's anyway. When some of our most important financial institutions have gone to the wall, or been expensively bailed out by taxpayers as a result of self-serving risk-taking by executives, it is safe to say that pens are no longer a pressing ethical issue.*

Half the firms surveyed in the UK are providing training in ethics and an increasing number are appointing 'ethics officers'. This is all very well, but the test comes when being 'ethical' conflicts with immediate business goals. Norman Bowie from the University of Minnesota – and author of A Kantian Theory of Leadership – applies the philosophical frameworks of the eighteenth-century philosopher Immanuel Kant to modern debates on ethical leadership. He quotes Kant's kingdom of ends formulation: 'One should act as if one were a member of an ideal kingdom of ends in which one was subject and sovereign at the same time.' Acting as if simultaneously sovereign and subject means that leaders should prepare decisions but not impose them. Here then is Bowie's Kantian leadership test: 'The leader enhances the autonomy of his or her followers.'

But it is inevitable that there will sometimes be a tension between a desire on the part of a business to be ethical and to be financially successful. A quarter of managers in the MORI survey agreed with the statement that 'it is acceptable to artificially increase profits in the books so long as no money is stolen'. Tell that to the workers who lose their pensions when the scheme unravels.

The power wielded by a CEO, their capacity to ruin or make lives, means that they have a disproportionate ethical responsibility. Cooking the books, or 'borrowing' from the pension fund to finance high-rolling overseas acquisition cannot be compared to borrowing a biro. For business leaders to win back the trust they have lost, ethics is more than a quick bolt-on or a new-fangled job title. It has to go to the heart of the way they create wealth – and why. 'I have had a few business leaders come to me and ask how they can restore trust,' says Bowie. 'We have had four *years of apparently unending scandals, which do seem to have had an impact... The days when the MBA was a master of the universe and the CEO was king are over – clearly they have now been knocked firmly off the pedestal.'*

At the new-age end of the spectrum, gurus such as Deepak Chopra suggest that the sources of wealth creation are moving from knowledge to wisdom. 'This shift in consciousness is the one single reality which affects all other realities,' he says.

Extraordinary leaders like Ray Anderson, who turned his firm Interface Carpets into an environmental beacon, are contemptuous of those who are unconvinced by the 'business case' for more ethical behaviour. 'I prefer to turn the question round,' he says. 'Where's the business case for double-glazing the planet? Or for destroying the coral reefs?'

In the end, ethics comes down to ethos – which is set by those with the most power in the organisation. A reliance on rules and regulations takes us only so far, as the 2008 crisis has demonstrated. 'What I would say is that it should go way beyond compliance,' says Bowie. 'What you need is a leader, a Warren Buffett type, a CEO who embodies an ethics culture.'

There are also dangers in 'professionalising' ethics. If ethics becomes a matter of following rules, the importance of doing the right thing – acting on 'gut instinct' – could be lost. In his polemic Alone Again: Ethics After Certainty, *sociologist Zygmunt Bauman suggests that rules can crush conscience and end up worsening matters: 'Conscience may tell that the action one was told to take is wrong – even if it is procedurally correct.' Using a rule for behaviour amounts to what he calls 'floating responsibility', in which the actions of an individual are justifiable against bureaucratic benchmarks.*

In Papering Over the Cracks – Rules, Regulation and Real Trust, *Edward Smith and Richard Reeves argue that self-regulation is followed in importance by peer regulation, market regulation and finally state regulation. None of this is to argue against clear, fair regulation by national governments and supranational bodies. But it is important to recognise that rules will always be bent, or innovated around, by the unscrupulous. In the end, it is moral reform as much as mechanical reform that is required to resuscitate capitalism.*

With the rise of 24/7 media and internet communications, direct action campaigns aimed squarely at corporate brands are likely to become highly effective. The campaign in 2006 against the US energy company TXU's plans to build 11 'dirty' coal-fired power stations in Texas is a good example. The protestors didn't just target TXU; they targeted the financiers of TXU. They went for Citibank, Morgan Stanley and Merrill Lynch. In carefully coordinated days of action, yellow tape was stuck across cash points, bearing the message 'global warming crime scene'. There were some high-profile stunts, including a mass 'die in' in the lobby of Merrill Lynch. Hollywood stars cut up their credit cards on TV.

The protest finally forced the new private equity owners to the negotiating table with the environmental lobby. The campaigners agreed to stop the protest and allow three plants to be built, on the condition that the company agreed to: scrap the other eight plants, along

with all coal-expansion plans in other states; endorse the US Climate Action Partnership, including its call for a mandatory federal cap on carbon emissions; reduce the company's carbon emissions to 1990 levels by 2020; increase spending on energy efficiency to $400 million; double TXU's investment in wind power; and honour the company's commitment to cut nitrogen oxides, sulphur dioxide and mercury by 20%. It was an extraordinary power shift – and has derailed the plans of other energy firms hoping to roll out coal-fired power stations.

Heightened awareness of the climate crisis is rapidly altering the desirability of certain products. Bottled water, for example, once a mark of prestige, is quickly acquiring pariah status because of the water and carbon that goes into its production. It may be that demand for red meat will drop once awareness of its environmental impact grows. According to the UN, 18% of global greenhouse emissions come from livestock production, more than all the cars, trucks and planes in the world. A kilo of beef requires between 50,000 and

100,000 litres of water. The average burping, farting cow produces more greenhouse gas than the average 4x4 car.

As well as looking out for ethical customers, smart companies are also becoming alert to the rise of 'ethical employees', who want their employers to be greener. A 2007 survey by Badenock and Clark, the professional services recruiter, found that 41% of employees said that they would be more likely to accept a job offer from a firm with strong green credentials, and that half felt that their current employer did not take environmental issues seriously. Climate-wrecking firms might soon become toxic employer brands, in the same way that tobacco companies are today.

Campaigners, customers, investors and employees are pressing on the conscience of companies. But in many cases the action is being driven from the boardroom, by a new breed of 'ethical CEOs'. They realise that the search for a cast-iron 'business case' for taking the right action on the environment is often futile, but that the action must be taken in any case. It's not yet clear how far ordinary consumers are voting with their wallets for greener products. Some chief executives now recognise that it is their responsibility to lead consumers, rather than the other way around.

WHAT IS TO BE DONE?

In 2007, the Chairman of the International Panel on Climate Change, Rajendra Pachauri, said: 'If there is no action before 2012, that's too late. What we do in the next two or three years will determine our future. This is the defining moment.' By our reckoning, that means that we are running out of time, fast.

Business leaders need to:

- **ASSESS THEIR EXPOSURE TO RISKS – PHYSICAL, REGULATORY AND REPUTATIONAL – FROM CLIMATE CHANGE**
- **MOVE TO FULL DISCLOSURE OF ENVIRONMENT IMPACTS, INCLUDING CARBON EMISSIONS**
- **SET DEMANDING INTERNAL TARGETS FOR CARBON REDUCTIONS**
- **LOBBY GOVERNMENTS FOR TOUGHER REGULATION TO ENSURE A LEVEL, GREEN PLAYING FIELD**

New leaders will also need to think differently about competition. New forms of collaboration are emerging. Retailers should continue to compete in terms of price and service, but there is every reason why they should work together in some areas, such as logistics. What's the point of one retailer having a half-empty lorry coming over from France, while a competitor does exactly the same? Why not share the lorry? Why not share the warehouse? Why not share the distribution networks? Similarly, firms can act in concert to improve supplier standards across the board, for example on greener packaging. Companies can bring down their carbon emissions by smart collaboration in the non-competitive elements of their business. This environmentally driven collaboration with competitors is called *co-opetition*, an essential skill for the executive of the future.

All MBA courses are about success of one sort or another. Most people undertaking an MBA – or reading this book – want to become more successful in terms of their own career: to earn more, acquire more power, have more impact. Great. We have absolutely no problem with these ambitions. We share them. *The 80 Minute MBA* contains advice on achieving success as a leader, a manager and a boss; success in creating workplaces full of energy and productivity; success in enriching your conversations with your customers and, of course, success in building piles of cash. But the post-2008 world requires us to reconfigure our notions of success. Not only to think about more robust, fairer forms of business and markets, but also to begin the patient, painful task of healing the planet. If success in any of those other domains comes at the cost of our children and grandchildren, then it is no kind of success worth having. Even the hardest-hearted are realising that green is the new black.

STATISTICS

Long and painful experience has taught me one great principle in managing business for other people, viz., if you want to inspire confidence, give plenty of statistics.

Three Years in a Curatorship by One Whom It Has Tried
C. L. Dodgson, 1886

I am distressed by a society which depends so completely on mathematics and science and yet seems so indifferent to the innumeracy ... of so many of its citizens.

Innumeracy: Mathematical Illiteracy and its Consequences
John Allen Paulos, 2001

It's self-evident that numeracy matters in life and business.

Few of us would try to get through life without tackling an inability to lift a glass of water to our mouth and drink from it without spilling anything. But, at least in part, that's what the majority of us do as we try to bluff our way through numerical neurosis.

Given the prevalence of this affliction, it is perhaps not surprising that many leading MBA programmes suggest that the least business-seasoned folk attend so-called 'maths camps' before they start the MBA course proper. Given that the need to attend a maths camp is probably caused by the fear-inducing inability to tackle simple maths problems, we're not sure the 'boot camp' approach adopts the right emotional tone.

Indeed, our experience suggests that in a prototype *'I'm an MBA student – get me out of here'* competition most MBA students would rather eat a witchetty grub or some kangaroo testicles than attend three days of maths boot camp.

Sometimes the most important skills in business are not enjoyable to acquire.

But why do numbers matter so much? Because they help us interpret the world around us and make decisions. If you can't do the maths, at least seek to understand what statistics tells you about how to use data to make discerning judgements. There are two key ideas in statistics that will equip you with those interpretative powers.

STATISTICAL SIGNIFICANCE

Accumulated research tells us that there is a statistically significant relationship between men who wear grey shoes and a general lack of discernment in all things. Alright, it doesn't, but let's assume for a moment it does (it should in a right-thinking world).

What does that mean? What is its significance?

It means that, in our example, the wearing of grey shoes and proven lack of discernment are related sufficiently strongly that they are not related by luck or chance. Which is where P values come in – a magic number in the world of statistics. P values capture the 'luck' relationship in observed differences between variables. They specify the level of luck we are prepared to tolerate before declaring that two variables are associated strongly and have a statistically significant relationship. The universal standard for statistical significance is when P is less than 0.05.

What does this figure mean? It means that when P is less than 0.05, there is a less than 5% chance that the relationship between two variables is due to luck or chance alone. Thus allowing us to say that there is a 'statistically significant' correlation between the two variables. But a strong, statistically significant relationship between two factors or variables doesn't imply one is causing the other.

CORRELATION AND CAUSATION

This leads us on to our second key idea in statistics – that correlation does not equal causation. A correlation simply means that a relationship exists between two factors – let's call them X and Y. It's possible that X causes Y – that causation is taking place – the one variable causing an observed difference in the other. But it may be that Y causes X. Or that some other factor, Z, is causing both X and Y – sometimes known as a *lurking variable*. A lurking variable is a variable that has an important effect on the relationship among the variables in a study but is not included among the variables studied.

Let's give you an example. Take the recent eye-catching headline opposite.[8]

The headline implies a causation connection. But with a few moments' thought it's easily rejected.

Bottled water linked to healthier babies

Affluent parents are more likely to buy and drink bottled water and have healthy children because they have the stability and material wherewithal to offer good food, clothing, shelter and amenities. Families with their own cappuccino makers are more likely to have healthier babies for the same reason. Affluence is the lurking variable.

None of which means that negative results, spurious correlations and causations aren't interesting. They can contain interesting information. Historically, academic journals have published only positive results – data showing one thing connected to another.

Bottled water   ➤   Healthier babies

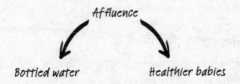

Affluence

Bottled water   Healthier babies

By not publishing negative results, generations of researchers can waste time and money repeating the same studies and finding the same unpublishable results. Step forward a recently launched social science journal, *The Journal of Spurious Correlations*, devoted exclusively to publishing negative results. We expect business research to make a major contribution to its pages in the future.[9]

LEADER-
SHIP

'My name is Ozymandias, king of kings:
Look on my works, ye Mighty, and despair!'
Nothing beside remains. Round the decay
Of that colossal wreck, boundless and bare,
The lone and level sands stretch far away.

'Ozymandias', Percy Bysshe Shelley

Here's the bad news: five books on leadership are published on a typical day. This torrent of advice on leadership is enough to provoke an anxiety attack in the staunchest executive. Now for some good news: the majority are so bad that they can be safely ignored. Bad books on leadership fall into one of two main categories. First, a famous business leader puts their photo on the front and writes a book with a single, dispiriting message: 'If Only You Were Me You'd Be As Famous And Successful As Me'. Second, a connection is made between leadership and a religion, organisation or fictional character. What can we learn about leadership from 'Moses CEO', the toys you loved as a child or US Navy SEALs? Answer: nothing.

Now for some properly bad news. In what will be seen as the halcyon years before 2008, the lamentable quality of most leadership advice didn't matter much. But now, as we collectively struggle to fix our broken financial system, the need for real reflection on what business leadership means is urgent. The necessary remoralisation of the market will place new ethical and personal demands on leaders. The cult of the CEO, overpaid and overconfident, has come to a shattering end. Business leaders now look like Shelley's Ozymandias, 'king of kings'. Their glittering city of a debt-fuelled, finance-driven capitalism has been razed – and leadership will never look quite the same again. Neither the Ancient Greeks nor early Christians would have been surprised by the events of 2008. The Athenians believed that insufficient humility before the gods – what they called *hubris* – would result in destructive forces being unleashed: the *nemesis*. This was a message reinforced in the Old Testament: 'Pride goes before destruction, and a haughty spirit before a fall' (Proverbs 16:18). Another verse of Proverbs explains why this is so: 'Every one who is arrogant is an abomination to the Lord; be assured, he will not go unpunished.'

Against this backdrop, the question 'Why should anyone be led by you?' acquires new force. It is the question asked by Rob Goffee and Gareth Jones, professors at the London Business School, in an influential article and book of that title. It is absolutely the right one. Anybody who aspires to lead must understand that the power of leaders stems, ultimately, from their followers. The motivation of the follower – the 'why' in the question – is critical. Power can be imposed upon people, but successful organisations need leaders who draw power out of others.

BOOKS TO IGNORE

Given the deluge of leadership advice, we want to help to guide your further reading by giving some areas to avoid. As a general rule, ignore books that put an adjective in front of the word 'leadership'. This will put plenty of books on your non-reading list – there is something of an adjectival arms race in this section of the market. Always keep in mind that a statement only has some value if a person can reasonably maintain the opposite. Leadership, it is variously argued, needs to be of the following kind:

- LIVING – RATHER THAN DEAD LEADERSHIP OR CORPSING LEADERSHIP, WHICH WE'VE ALL EXPERIENCED AT SOME POINT IN OUR CAREER
- COURAGEOUS – DEFINITELY BETTER THAN COWARDLY!
- SPIRITUAL – RATHER THAN, SAY, RADICAL ATHEIST LEADERSHIP
- RESONANT – AS OPPOSED TO DISSONANT. FACED WITH THE CHOICE BETWEEN THE TWO, WHO DOESN'T WANT TO RESONATE?
- PRIMAL – RATHER THAN, SAY, SECONDARY. (ACTUALLY THIS ONE IS PERHAPS THE EXCEPTION TO THE AVOID ADJECTIVES RULE, SINCE IT'S ACTUALLY RATHER GOOD, IN SPITE OF THE TITLE)
- SERVANT – BRITISH PM TONY BLAIR DECLARED IN 1997 'WE ARE THE SERVANTS NOW.' YEAH, RIGHT
- LIQUID – OF COURSE HUMANS ARE MOSTLY WATER, WHICH HELPS. BUT YOU MUST AVOID BEING TOO SOLID. AND GASEOUS LEADERSHIP IS WORST OF ALL

STUFF TO FORGET

Leadership books and theories can be daunting. Readers are often left with the impression that they need to be good at everything, to be a superperson who is intellectually strong, emotionally literate, decisive yet understanding, charismatic and down-to-earth, visionary and realistic. So we want to give you a whole bunch of things to stop worrying about. Here's a list of common leadership attributes or skills which are not worth spending much time on: charisma, balance, authenticity, coaching and strategy. Some brief explanation is probably in order.

CHARISMA

You can forget about charisma for two reasons. First, there's no evidence that charismatic leaders are more successful – if anything, the opposite may be true. Second, charisma cannot be taught or learned. If you're not charismatic, you are never going to be. So forget about it.

BALANCE

Businesses often apply a 'balanced scorecard' approach to the capacities of their staff. The Human Resources profession leapt on the idea with some enthusiasm in the 1990s. This is a misuse of the original idea, which stemmed from an article in the *Harvard Business Review* in 1992 by Robert Kaplan and David Norton. For the originators, the balanced scorecard was a range of things which a firm should be monitoring in order to check its health and performance: 'Think of the balanced scorecard as the dials and indicators in an aeroplane cockpit. For the complex task of navigating and flying an aeroplane, pilots need detailed information about many aspects of the flight.' On an organisational level, this is a sound approach. But not when it is applied to individuals. One of the things you can be sure of is that you are rubbish at certain things, and you will *always* be rubbish at certain things. You are unbalanced. If you spend all your time trying to get better at the things at which you're intrinsically rubbish, you won't get on with the job of being a leader. Great leaders are necessarily unbalanced; they just *know* they are.

AUTHENTICITY

Well, OK, on the face of it it's better to be authentic, right? But dig a bit deeper into the literature on authentic leadership and it's a bit less obvious than it sounds. There is some valuable thinking on this subject. But there are dangers too. One is that authentic leadership gets confused with honesty. You all know there are plenty of times when the right thing to do is lie. Examples might be: 'Are you thinking of leaving before we go bankrupt?' or 'Are we for sale?' Winston Churchill's diaries make it clear that in 1940 he didn't think America was going to come into the war, that the Germans looked overwhelming in terms of the numbers and that Britain was almost certainly going to go down. But he did not stand up and say that in the House of Commons. He did not go on the radio and say: 'My fellow citizens, we're all toast. Run for the hills.' He said something inspiring: we'll beat them, we're going to win, etc. He lied, but he lied very well, very successfully. Was he, then, an authentic leader? Perhaps not. Was he a great leader? Yes.

Goffee and Jones, the most thoughtful advocates of authentic leadership, recognise that there are tensions. Authentic leaders are those who 'reveal their weaknesses'. But the trouble is that this could undermine authority, so they need to be selective: 'Knowing which weakness to disclose is a highly honed art... A leader should reveal only a tangential flaw or perhaps even several of them. Paradoxically, this admission will help divert attention away from major weaknesses.' But Goffee and Jones stress that this is a very difficult task, 'especially when the end result must be authenticity'.

It is clearly better to 'be yourself' on most occasions, and this is where the idea of authenticity has some force. But because leadership requires a kind of 'selective authenticity' – which comes perilously close to an oxymoron – it is better to avoid the ambition. Niccolo Machiavelli, who has won the rare historical distinction of having his name turned into an adjective, is worth reconsidering in this respect. Being Machiavellian does not mean acting in a self-serving fashion. The ultimate goal is not power, but *glory* – and glory not only for the Prince of his title, but for the state as a whole. To this end, Machiavelli endorses strategic dissimulation. We agree.

COACHING

As a way of getting your company to pay for your therapy, coaching is a brilliant idea. Society would run much better if more of us took the time to consider our motivations, dreams and inner obstacles. Good coaching is like good counselling: it provides people with the time, tools, support and space to make positive changes in their life. But there is no good evidence that firms which invest in coaching for their high-flyers are more successful as a result, even if the individual gains from it. This might be because coaching is an unregulated market, so that any cowboy with a well-modulated voice can set up as a coach. Whether or not leaders benefit from coaching, we seriously doubt if a 'coaching style' of leadership is to be striven for. The sort of skills needed by a good coach tend not to be the same as the skills of a leader. In particular, a good coach must be neutral about the goals being pursued by an individual: their job is to help the coachee to achieve them. A leader, by contrast, must be clear about what a subordinate should be trying to achieve.

STRATEGY

Last but not least, don't worry about strategy. We are aware that this is a slightly controversial statement: most MBAs spend months on strategy. So we'll spend a tiny bit longer on this one (see the box below). But if you're already half-convinced, here's the short version: it's not making strategy that counts, it's putting it into practice. As Elvis wisely put it, 'A little less conversation, a little more action'.

STRATEGY

There's a deadly truth about strategy. It's nearly always over-resourced inside organisations. Why? Because too many businesses have a silver bullet delusion *about strategy – gripped by the notion that if we just get our strategy perfect we'll differentiate ourselves and beat the competition. Unfortunately, strategy is nowhere near as important as some organisations and leaders think it is.*

Of course it matters.

In their excellent book Hard Facts, Dangerous Half-Truths and Total Nonsense: Profiting from Evidence-Based Management, *Jeffrey Pfeffer and Robert Sutton encourage you to imagine a business as a collection of iron filings on a piece of paper. A good strategy lines them up, establishing common purpose and directing resources behind a clear set of goals. It tells organisations what to focus on and, almost as importantly, what not to do. But organisations should stop chasing the perfect strategy. The key differentiator for business, what makes the difference between successful and less successful, is the ability to execute. Richard Kovacevic, reflecting on his*

---

successful tenure as CEO at Norwest, had this to say about the relative importance of strategy and execution: 'I could leave our strategic plan on a plane and it wouldn't make any difference. No one could execute it. Our success has nothing to do with planning. It has to do with execution.'[1]

A 'good enough' strategy well executed is worth a hundred times more than a great strategy badly executed. As Larry Bossidy and Ram Charam argue in their book Execution: The Discipline of Getting Things Done, *leaders are spending too much time strategising, philosophising and pontificating. 'People think of execution as the tactical side of the business,' they write, 'something leaders delegate while they focus on the perceived "bigger issues". This idea is completely wrong.' Bear in mind that execution is the major task of a business leader and this becomes a pretty damning statement.*

So why is strategy such a resistant creature inside businesses?

Let's reveal the real terrible secret about strategy. For leaders and MBA students, strategy is the activity where they can still feel powerful in a world where they increasingly don't feel powerful. Strategy-making has therefore become the required caffeine hit for an active executive team. It suits business leaders to talk endlessly about 'disruption' and 'revolution', about game-changing new technologies which demand a new response. Yet the evidence of the last ten years, as the impact of internet technology has played out across business, is that the majority of companies winning on the internet use the new technology to leverage and execute their existing strategy better.[2]

Let's not forget: strategy-making is fun. It's easy for clever people, and you feel in charge. It's an extreme sport for executives without the risk of breaking any bones. In our experience, strategy and hardship are never corporate bedfellows. 'Strategy away days' and 'spa hotels' normally feature in the same sentence. But we shouldn't be too critical. It's tough at the top. Executives need the odd break. And strategy away days really deliver. And they're a damn sight easier than executing.

HEROES

One of our greatest business heroes is an unassuming man called Darwin E. Smith. Darwin was the Chief Executive of Kimberly-Clark from 1971 to 1991. When Darwin took over, KC was a struggling paper company. Here is the firm's performance BD (Before Darwin):

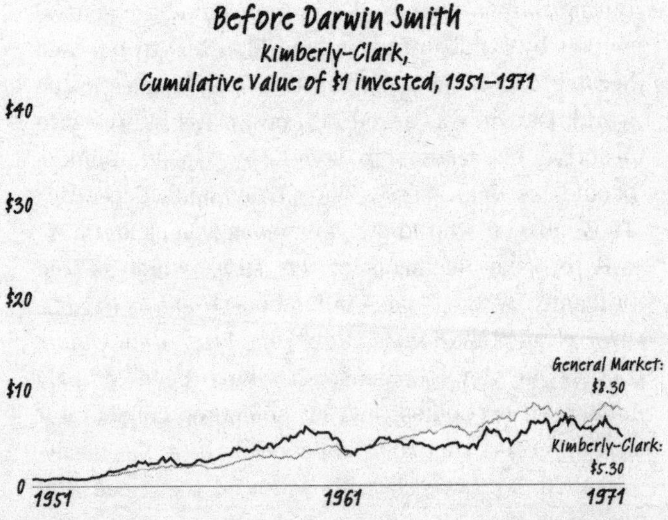

Before Darwin Smith
Kimberly-Clark,
Cumulative Value of $1 invested, 1951–1971
$40
$30
$20
$10
0
General Market:
$8.30
Kimberly-Clark:
$5.30
1951
1961
1971

In the years BD, Kimberly-Clark was, if anything, actually slightly underperforming in the general market. Now look at the years AD:

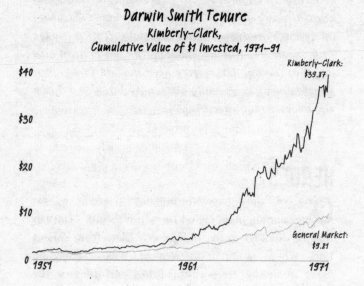

Darwin Smith Tenure
Kimberly-Clark,
Cumulative Value of $1 invested, 1951–91

During Darwin's tenure, KC outperformed the general market by a ratio of something like four to one and became one of the most successful companies in the world. Darwin was asked in a rare press interview to describe his leadership style. He paused, blinked behind his thick glasses and finally said, 'Eccentric'. Those of you who know your management literature will recognise elements of this story, which is told brilliantly by Jim Collins in his book *Good to Great – Why Some Companies Make the Leap and Others Don't*. Our views on leadership have been strongly influenced by Collins (and his sometime collaborator Jerry Porras). Actually, 'influenced' is a bit mealy-mouthed; we have slavishly followed their lead. But here's the thing: we think Collins's research is sound and his conclusions robust. His findings are also borne out by our own experience of working with leaders and leadership teams. We love Collins. We are unashamed Collins groupies.

One of the reasons for our admiration is that Collins derives his conclusions from carefully assembled data – even when he doesn't find what they were looking for. In *Good to Great*, Collins was looking to see what made some companies exhibit a step-change in performance. Overleaf is the trajectory of the 11 he identified.

Collins was not looking for leadership attributes to explain the change in direction. In fact, because lazy researchers often retreat to a mantra of 'it must be the leadership' to explain differences in performance, Collins told his team not to focus on the boss. But the data was unequivocal. The quality of the CEO turned out to be a critical factor in explaining why a company became great: the 11 companies identified outperformed the market, on average, by a factor of seven in the 15 years after an obvious 'transition point' in performance.

Smith thought himself eccentric, but in fact his approach bore a strong resemblance to that of the other ten leaders: George Cain, Alan Wurtzel, David Maxwell, Colman Mockler, Jim Herring, Lyle Everingham, Joe Cullman, Fred Allen, Cork Walgreen and Carl Reichhardt. Don't worry if you haven't heard of them either; it reveals not your ignorance, but their wisdom. In retirement, Smith explained, 'I never stopped trying to become qualified for the job.'

THE GOOD-TO-GREAT STUDY

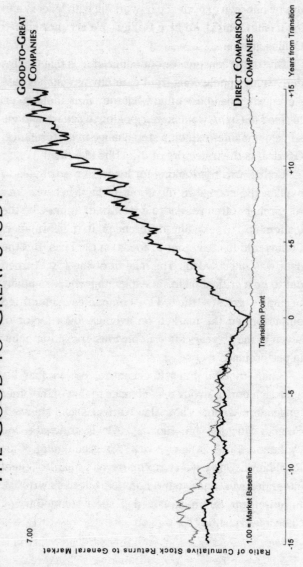

Shows average ratio, each company set to 1.00 at transition date.

THE LEADERSHIP WIKI: FOUR THINGS GREAT LEADERS KNOW

Being a successful leader is less about who you are or what you do than about what you know. The term 'wiki' stands for 'what I know is' and a successful leader's internal wiki includes four key pieces of knowledge: *where* the organisation is heading; *what* is going on; *who* they are; and *how* to build a strong team.

WHERE WE'RE GOING

The first thing successful leaders know is where the organisation is going. This sounds obvious, but that's not always the case. Plenty of nominal leaders subscribe to the approach satirised by the nineteenth-century French radical Alexandre Ledru-Rollin as: 'There go my people. I must find out where they're going, so that I can lead them.' Take our hero Darwin E. Smith. When he took over Kimberly-Clark, he realised that the future of the firm lay not in paper, but in paper products like tissues, diapers and paper towels. That's where the margin was. This meant that the firm no longer needed to own its own paper mill, so he said that they would sell it. Not an easy call, given the location of the mill: Kimberly. That's a big, bold decision. But Smith made it very clear from the outset: *that's* where we're going; we're getting out of *this* market and into *that* market – and he never deviated from that view. Everyone knew where the organisation was going. A key ingredient in the culture of a successful organisation is that everyone knows its destination – its animating purpose – and, crucially, the contribution of their own efforts. (This is a theme we pick up in the section on Culture.)

Charles R. 'Cork' Walgreen, who ran the family firm Walgreen's from 1971 to 1998, made a similar decision to take the firm out of food-service operations and focus on pharmacies. His successor, Dan Jorndt, recalled how, after months of discussion, Cork announced at a board meeting: 'OK, now I am going to draw a line in the sand. We are going to be out of the restaurant business completely in five years.' According to Jorndt, 'You could have heard a pin drop.' Not surprising, given that at the time the firm had over 500 restaurants. But the direction was crystal clear, and Jorndt reported that Cork 'never doubted; never second-guessed'. At a planning meeting six months later, a manager repeated the aim of shedding the restaurants within five years. Cork said: 'Listen, you have four a half years. I said you had five years six months ago. Now you've got four and half years.' This incident had a galvanising effect: the whole organisation quickly understood that he actually meant five years. One of the most commonly reported failings of leaders is, paradoxically, an unwillingness to use their authority. This is not a problem with the leaders whose organisations are most successful. They are not bullying or hectoring, but they are authoritative. Authority without arrogance: that's the secret.

WHAT'S GOING ON?

Successful leaders build, in Collins's phrase, a 'culture of discipline'. They are about getting things done, managing information effectively in order to control costs and marshal resources. If this sounds a little unglamorous for the titans of the corporate world, this is because of the unfortunate division made in recent years between leadership and its slightly grubby cousin, management. The business analyst Warren Bennis wrote: 'Management is about doing things right; leadership is about doing the right things.' It was a much-repeated sentence, and an unhelpful one. Pretty soon, people such as Liz Cook and Brian Rothwell were arguing that 'Management is a science; leadership is an art.'

The trouble with the leadership/management dichotomy is that it lets bosses off the hook when it comes to constructing good management information systems and scrutinising the results – tracking the development of projects, peering into departmental accounts and generally keeping their arms around the organisation. Once leaders start talking about 'keeping their eyes on the horizon' or taking a 'helicopter view', sell your shares and/or start looking for a new job. As the business writers Bruce Pasternak and James O'Toole correctly lament: 'We now know many companies have been overled and undermanaged.' Leaders were so busy being 'strategic', that half the time they didn't know what the heck was going on in their own organisations.

The 11 successful leaders from *Good to Great* were the sort who were happier spending their evening with the monthly management accounts than at a swanky New York dinner. You *do* have to sweat the small stuff.

Great leaders also keep in touch with how people are feeling. Successful leaders do not spend their whole time worrying if everyone is happy. But they do know what the emotional temperature of the organisation is. The excellent work by Daniel Goleman and his colleagues on emotional intelligence or EQ (which includes *Primal Leadership*) shows that good leaders are emotionally in tune with the people in their organisation. Knowledgeable leaders understand that people are not machines to be reprogrammed according to the latest strategy document. In particular, they understand that change provokes an emotional response, and that successful change involves allowing people some space to feel angry, resentful and afraid as well as excited, hopeful and energised.

In her insightful book *The Change Monster*, Jeanie

Daniel Duck describes the emotional rollercoaster that characterises profound organisational change, and how a failure to allow for the emotional aspects of change scuppers the entire enterprise. As Duck writes, 'Emotions are data. In any transformation, there are common patterns that can be identified and accurately analyzed with real rigor and rationality. With understanding, there are a variety of ways to address potential problems successfully.' But it is important not to confuse EQ with a need for constant soul-searching. Leaders need to be open and emotionally sentient. But nobody is going to follow a self-scrutinising wimp.

WHO AM I?

Successful leaders know who they are. They know where they're strong. But they know their weaknesses too. There's a fierce humility to successful leaders. They know they can't do x, y and z. They do not presume that they are all-conquering. They are willing to hire people as talented or more talented than themselves to fill senior positions around them.

A realistic assessment of personal performance provides a vital clue to leadership potential. In an important article, 'What We Know About Leadership', psychologists Robert Hogan, Gordon Curphy and Joyce Hogan summarised a substantial body of research comparing the assessments by leaders of their own performance with the views of their colleagues. The leaders whose self-appraisal matched the judgement of those working for them were the ones who were most likely to succeed, while those who overrated themselves were far and away the worst leaders. So if you think you're God's gift, we recommend conducting an anonymous survey among your staff, just to check that they concur. The best research on leadership also suggests that the experts in assessing and predicting leadership potential are not expensive consultants with complex models and 'assessment centres', but peers and subordinates.

Those who become successful leaders tend to be socially skilled too, able to pick up on social cues in their interactions and 'judge the mood' accurately. Leaders who fail – and at least half suffer from what US researchers graphically dub 'executive derailment' – are generally not lacking technical skill, ambition or intelligence. It's their character that lets them down. As Hogan and his colleagues write: 'Many managers who are bright, hard-working, ambitious, and technically competent fail (or are in danger of failing) because they are perceived as arrogant, vindictive, untrustworthy, selfish, emotional, compulsive, overcontrolling, insensitive, abrasive, aloof, too ambitious, or unable to delegate or make decisions.' And that's on a good day.

The successful leaders of the *Good to Great* companies were, says Collins, 'a study in duality: modest and wilful, humble and fearless'. The individuals were fairly humble about themselves, but not about their organisations: they combined 'personal humility with intense professional will'. Most importantly, they cared about the success of their organisations, rather than their own personal success. It's not about getting on the front cover of *Fortune* magazine or being active on the speaker circuit. For them, it is not about being a great business leader, but about leading a great business. More than 1,000 years ago, the author of *Beowulf*, the epic Anglo-Saxon tale, wrote: 'Behaviour that's admired is the path to power among people everywhere.' It is important, then, for us all to admire the right kinds of behaviour in our leaders.

HOW TO BUILD A STRONG TEAM

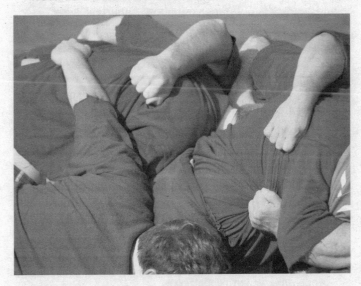

Successful leaders are motivated by what they *build* rather than what they *get*. Most importantly, great leaders build great teams. They surround themselves with talented people – people with talents that they do not possess themselves and know they do not. As President Harry S. Truman reminded us, 'You can accomplish anything in life, provided you do not mind who gets the credit.'

This is one of the reasons why their companies continue to succeed long after they've gone. Very often, strong leaders build the team first, then decide where to go. With the right people, you can go to different, better places. We have said that great leaders have a clear sense of direction, of where the organisation is going. But very often this is the result of collective decision-making in a talented team. Because the future holds so much uncertainty, a team with the agility to retask, seize new opportunities and question received wisdom is more important than a single dominant vision. 'The old adage "People are your most important asset" is wrong,' says Collins. 'People are not your most important asset. The *right* people are.' In practice, this means:

- DON'T COMPROMISE IN HIRING PEOPLE. HOLD OUT FOR THE BEST RATHER THAN SIMPLY PLUGGING THE GAP

- IF SOMEONE DOESN'T WORK OUT, DON'T DILLY-DALLY. ONCE IT IS CLEAR THAT THEY DON'T FIT THE FIRM (RATHER THAN THE SPECIFIC JOB), THEY HAVE TO GO

- ENCOURAGE DEBATE, DISSENT AND ARGUMENT IN THE TOP TEAM. IF YOU'VE GOT THE RIGHT PEOPLE THEY WILL WANT THEIR SAY, BUT ALSO BE WILLING TO PUT THEIR WEIGHT BEHIND THE AGREED APPROACH

- COMMUNICATE, COMMUNICATE, COMMUNICATE. TEAMS WORK BEST WHEN THEIR MEMBERS ARE WELL-INFORMED. IF IN DOUBT, SHARE YOUR THINKING WITH YOUR TEAM

- SPEND A LOT OF TIME ON ROLES AND RESPONSIBILITIES. TALENTED PEOPLE DON'T NEED MUCH MANAGEMENT, SO LONG AS THEY ARE A SQUARE PEG IN A SQUARE HOLE. COLMAN MOCKLER, CEO OF GILLETTE FROM 1975 TO HIS DEATH IN 1991, SAID, 'EVERY MINUTE DEVOTED TO PUTTING THE PROPER PERSON IN THE PROPER SLOT IS WORTH WEEKS OF TIME LATER'

- ENERGISE YOUR PEOPLE. ENERGY IS PERHAPS THE MOST IMPORTANT INGREDIENT OF ORGANISATIONAL SUCCESS, AND GOOD LEADERS ARE ENERGISERS. (WE SPEND SOME MORE TIME ON ENERGY IN THE NEXT CHAPTER)

HURRY SICKNESS

Successful leadership takes time. Time to know yourself and colleagues. Time to make good hiring and firing decisions. But time may feel like the scarcest resource of all. You may be suffering from what James Gleick, in his book Faster: The Acceleration of Just About Everything, *calls hurry sickness. Here's a Hurry Sickness Test, adapted from Gleick – a quick one, of course, which you can administer to yourself.*

- *When you brush your teeth in the morning, are you always doing something else at the same time – finding underwear, choosing a shirt, yelling at the kids?*

- *When you just catch a train or a plane – jumping on a moment before the doors close – do you secretly get a kick out of it? Is it worth missing the odd one to get that rush, to enjoy the feeling of having wasted a nanosecond with all the losers in the departure lounge?*

- *When you get into a lift, do you immediately look for the 'door-close' button? You're not alone. 'It gets more used than any other button in the elevator,' says John Kendall, Director of Advanced Technology at Otis Elevator Company. 'When they're in the elevator they want to go.' This is despite the fact that the delay – technically known as 'door dwell' (see, it's just dwelling) – is between two and four seconds. Four seconds? It's unimaginable you'd wait that long, isn't it?*

- *When you call a lift and it all looks good – the button makes a 'bing' noise, the light comes on and stays on – do you, if it does not arrive within a certain period of time, go back and press the button again? Thought so. One of our clients said, 'No I don't go back and press it again: I HOLD IT DOWN.' Now, if you think this action will in fact speed the arrival of the lift, we can't help you. Although at least you are behaving rationally. The rest of you are doing something you know to be irrational. Why? Because it's killing you. Those 10, 15, 20 seconds are killing you.*

Count how many questions you answered yes to.

Scores:
0 = So laid-back, you are virtually horizontal. Time to get a job?
1 = Buddhist levels of hurry health.
2 = Not too bad at all; you control time well.
3 = Early symptoms of hurry sickness.
4 = Chasing your own tail most of the day, advanced stages of the disease.
5 = Whoa! Slow down tiger! (Or buy a portable defibrillator.)

We are acutely aware that discussing the dangers of hurry sickness in the context of The 80 Minute MBA *is ironic or paradoxical or – yes, alright – downright hypocritical. Guilty as charged. We should indeed heal ourselves. But we can all surely agree about the danger of confusing business with busyness; of packing our diaries with meetings in order to avoid*

One way to test the 'teaminess' of a leader is their attitude towards succession. Great leaders want great successors, and usually find them within their own ranks, rather than in the 'global marketplace' for CEOs. But a selfless attitude to succession does not come easily to all. Management expert Manfred Kets de Vries writes: 'I've often said, tongue in cheek, that the major task of a CEO is to find his most likely successor and kill the bastard.' Less successful leaders are those who take a certain delight in the way the company crashed after they left. They can then say, 'Well, it was all about me then, wasn't it? Look what happened as soon as I left.' *Après moi le déluge.* What better evidence for your own brilliance than the crashing and burning of the next in line? 'It is not enough to succeed', Gore Vidal reminds us. 'Others must also fail.'

In this sense, Jack Welch – who we bet you *have* heard of – is an anti-hero of business leadership. It is undeniable that General Electric performed strongly when he was at the helm, not least because of his intense focus on cost-cutting and throwing out the weakest-performing staff (although it is worth pointing out that the *Good to Great* companies did much better). In an interview with the *Financial Times* in July 2008, Welch said, 'You can look at it any way you want and I don't care what you say. We had 425,000 employees and $25bn of business. When I left we had 310,000 and $125bn, five times the revenue, 25 per cent fewer people.' The comment reveals Welch's considerable belief in his own abilities. His talk is not about the skills of the team around him, or of needing to continue to learn anything himself. When GE missed some important targets following his departure, Welch went on TV to warn that he would 'shoot' Jeff Immelt, his successor, if he did not rectify the 'screw-up'. (Welch retracted the following day, but it was an insight into his mindset.)

The finest leaders are those with bigger ambitions for their organisation than for themselves. They know that the greatest strength of an organisation lies with its people, and in its *culture* – the focus of our next chapter.

CULTURE

> Far and away the best prize that life offers is the chance to work hard at work worth doing.
>
> Theodore Roosevelt, 1903 Labor Day Address

We've never been very fond of the phrase *human resources*. It conjures up dusty images of administration-obsessed personnel functions, and the 'human remains' jibes have definitely damaged the brand. *Culture* is a better way of framing the challenge of people and organisations – encouraging a necessary focus on how to make our workplace cultures fit for purpose and fulfilling for employees and enterprises alike.

It is a self-evident truth that organisations need to care about their culture. People are simultaneously the most valuable factor of production and the most difficult to engage effectively. Not many organisations operate as if they have accepted either of these inconvenient truths.

PEOPLE = VALUE^x

Let's start with the most familiar workplace cliché: 'People are our greatest asset.' The two questions that should be posed in response are:

Do leaders mean it?

Is it true?

To which the answers are:

Leaders often't don't – or at least not enough.

But it is true.

In our experience, most senior executives – despite their public protestations to the contrary – are not fully convinced that the ultimate success of their firm depends on how well they manage, engage and invest in their people. To be fair, this is partly because it has proved difficult to establish clear, irrefutable evidence that investments in the workforce boost business performance.

But it also reflects the fact that CEOs find it easier to influence – and therefore put their personal faith in – new business strategies or marketing plans. Their meddling must make a material difference right now. The process of engaging employees is often too time-consuming and the performance payback too slow for an impatient CEO.

But it is quite clear that the labour, or what economists call *human capital*, has a unique ability to create value in the modern economy. As we've moved from an industrial to a knowledge economy, 'hard' physical assets, such as buildings and machinery, have become less important (though of course still vital in many sectors). *Intangible assets* – non-monetary assets that cannot be seen, touched or physically measured, such as intellectual property, innovation and knowledge – are the motors of value inside modern enterprises. They now account for up to 80% of the value of large companies.[1] In straight economic terms, people contribute more value to businesses than any other factor of production.

Knowledge workers now make up 42% of the

workforce in the UK, up from 31% in 1984.[2] Investment patterns have followed suit. Recent US evidence suggests that business investment in intangible assets started to accelerate from the 1980s onwards, exceeding investment in tangibles by 36% by the early 2000s.[3]

COMMITMENT SEEKERS

The stakes have therefore been raised on the people front. The mini-industries that have grown up around the so-called 'war for talent' and offering *employee engagement* solutions reflect companies' desire to get more from their people. What makes human capital special – its humanity – also makes it harder to coordinate and inspire. You don't hear managers complaining about lazy steel rods. The holy grail for organisations – and the factor which often separates successful organisations from the rest – is getting people voluntarily to give more of their best.

It's what we call the *commitment dividend.*

The commitment dividend comes from employees who care about the organisation's aims, who willingly make improvements, contribute ideas and take decisions – all symptoms of high levels of discretionary commitment. Managers talk about employees who are prepared to work 'beyond contract' – in other words, their commitment to the job extends beyond the narrow confines of their job description. But this is not just about motivating individuals. Successful teams and organisations are greater than the sum of their parts. The strength of the relationships and networks – the *social capital* – in the firm is a key determinant of productivity.

It is, by now, hopefully even more blindingly clear

that people matter. The economics of human capital make this truth stark. And the point is not simply that the work of people is intrinsically more valuable, but also that the harder they work and the better they work together – commitment dividend plus social capital – the more successful the organisation will be.

So what do we do about that? How do we motivate people? How do we engage employees? Money, perks and physical environment count for relatively little. Or rather, getting them wrong is seriously demotivating, but getting them right is not what lights a fire inside people. They are what the influential management theorist Frederick Herzberg calls 'maintenance' or 'hygiene' factors. What actually releases the commitment dividend – the factors Herzberg calls 'motivational factors' – are more to do with quality of relationships, levels of individual discretion and the prevailing organisational ethos. As Herzberg puts it: 'If you want someone to do a good job, give them a good job to do.' There is a considerable literature on reward systems and performance-related pay. We would not recommend spending too much time in this particular thicket. The goal should not be a high-tech reward system, but rewarding work.

FORMING CULTURES

First though, a quick word on the way organisational cultures are created, sustained and altered. All MBAs will contain a 'culture change' module. But this language is not quite right. Organisational cultures, rather like mould, grow. Of course, they grow in new directions, sometimes as a result of deliberate executive intent, more often as a consequence of historical accident and fate. And organisational cultures are highly resistant to 'culture change' programmes, consultants and projects. It is not big-change programmes that change culture, but the accumulation of thousands of small actions – what are sometimes known as *micro behaviours* – over time. Behaviours are the threads of any social fabric. The philosopher Gerry Cohen, writing on social justice in his marvellously titled book *If You're an Egalitarian, How Come You're So Rich?*, puts it like this: 'I now believe that a change in social ethos, a change in the attitudes people sustain towards each other in the thick of daily life, is necessary for producing equality.' We love that phrase 'in the thick of daily life'. Because it is in the thick of everyday working life that cultures are created – or destroyed.

There are plenty of firms which declare themselves in favour of flexible working and work/life balance, but all the manager has to do is glance at his watch as you leave, or make a 'joke' about being a part-timer when you come in late, or roll their eyes when you say you'd like to work from home. There are plenty of firms that stress their commitment to gender equality, but in which staff stick a *Nuts* screensaver on their computer, or request a 'busty blonde' for a client call. There are plenty of organisations that proudly declare their green credentials, but then fly the entire senior management to the Mediterranean for an annual strategy session, aka knees-up.

And the more senior and powerful an individual is, the greater the impact of their own behaviour – for good and for ill. Apologies for the obviousness of this statement. But we have been struck by the number of senior executives who claim that a particular course of action is not possible because 'the culture round here won't allow it'. To which the response has to be: but it's *your* culture. As a senior manager or executive, you have a huge impact on the culture simply through the way you conduct yourself each day. For example, a number of workplace studies have shown the sizeable impact of a boss saying 'thank you'. The more senior a position a person holds, the more power they have to shape the culture and climate of their organisation. This is a power which too few leaders take seriously enough.

What kind of culture, then, should managers try to help create? A successful organisational culture has three key features: solidarity, energy and autonomy.

SOLIDARITY

Solidarity sounds like a powerful Polish trade union from the 1980s. And of course it is, one which under the leadership of Lech Walesa – who went on to become President of Poland – played a significant role in bringing about the end of the communist regime in that nation and helped to spark the 1989 revolutions across Eastern Europe. But if it seems like an odd word, we think it's the right one. Solidarity captures two related factors: *community* and *purpose*. Solidarity means that 'we're all in this together'.

A community is built upon sociability. Small surprise, then, that the most consistently powerful predictor of job satisfaction is the answer to the following question: 'Do you have a close friend at work?' Having a pal at work is vital to a sense of sociability. This finding should be put alongside the evidence that people most often cite their relationship with their immediate superior as a reason for quitting. 'Toxic Bosses' remain one of US employees' biggest problems at work, according to a recent *Business Week* survey.[4] The importance of relationships is clear:

people stay for their mates, and leave because of their managers.

Sociable workplaces are those where gossiping by the water cooler is not seen as a semi-criminal activity; where investments are made in physical spaces for people to interact; and in which the Christmas party is never, ever cancelled.

Communities are built on relationships, which in turn are built on *conversations*. Most organisations are now over-communicating with themselves – not least because of the ease of e-mail – but under-conversing. As Theodore Zeldin argues in *Conversation* (a brilliant book), conversations can go 'off-agenda', lead anywhere, mix up diverse topics and are conducted without hierarchy. Conversations are the synapses of the organisational brain – spaces in which sparks are ignited. (They are also the way smart firms conduct their relationships with other vital stakeholders, including customers, as we'll argue later.)

But, of course, organisations are not just running a kind of social club, a place to sit with a cappuccino, flirt, and talk about the weekend. There's stuff to do, a common purpose to be pursued. That's what solidarity means: a community with a purpose.

In the previous chapter, we discussed the importance of leaders being able to establish a clear sense of purpose and direction: to know and communicate where the organisation is going. People need to know what the organisation is trying to achieve, but also how what they're doing on a day-to-day basis contributes to that goal. You have probably heard the story of the NASA cleaner, who when asked by a visiting bigwig – perhaps even a president (JFK or LBJ) – 'What do you do?' answers, 'I help to put men on the moon.' This story may well be apocryphal – at any rate, we cannot source it satisfactorily. The fact that there is a similar story about a stone-mason, Christopher Wren and St Paul's Cathedral makes us even more sceptical. But the tale continues to be told because it is a perfect example of a worker seeing a clear connection between their day job and the organisation's overall purpose. There is a clear *line of sight* between daily, individual exertion and long-term, collective goals.

But what very often happens is that at some point in the organisation, that line of sight is lost, so that people feel as if they're shovelling bits of paper around, adding up columns of numbers or cleaning toilets, none of which appears to connect with the purpose of the organisation.

ENERGY

For many years the most evocative description of a company culture was the phrase coined by the London Business School's late, great Professor Sumantra Ghoshal: 'the smell of the place'. We've always struggled a bit with this. The smell of a place can depend on the state of the air-conditioning or the volume of perfume on a receptionist. It seems to us that energy is a better way of capturing the essence of an organisation's soul. Never mind the smell: feel the vibe.

We're not huge Jack Welch fans, to be honest. We much prefer Darwin E. Smith. But Welch does capture, in his '4 Es of Leadership', some of the most important ways in which leaders shape their organisations' culture. The first two Es are 'positive energy' – working with enthusiasm and enjoyment – and 'the ability to energize others… to get other people revved up'. (The other two Es are 'edge', or 'the courage to make tough yes-or-no decisions', and 'execute – the ability to get the job done'.) Welch is absolutely right. A CEO of a major publishing company we've worked with said to us, 'I've come to the conclusion that my job is simply injecting energy into the right part of the organisation at the right time.'

DRAINS AND RADIATORS

In life, there are people who are *drains* and those who are *radiators*. If you go out for a drink for an hour with a drain, you'll need another drink afterwards to recover. They've drained your energy out of you. Your battery level's flat-lined. But spend an hour with a radiator and you'll end up with a bit more of a spring in your step yourself. They've energised you. (Hopefully you haven't drained it all out of them.) Think about the drains and radiators in your life. Worry quite a bit if your spouse falls into the former category. As a leader, part of your job is to keep the energy levels up. We don't mean a cocaine-fuelled, mass hysteria kind of energy. But there is a distinct hum to successful teams. Your own interactions with your team should release energy.

But institutional practices can also act as drains or radiators. A useful exercise is simply to ask people what these are in your organisation. Does the 'motivational' session raise energy levels? Or is it something else? What depletes energy? Meetings are a commonly cited example. This is why meetings always have biscuits and coffee in them. The mere fact of being in a meeting is draining the energy out of the participants so quickly that they have to shove it back in – in the form of sugar and caffeine – simply in order to survive for the next hour. Find out where the radiators and drains are located in your organisation and see whether or not it's possible to improve levels of energy. And guard your own energy levels: if you're running on empty, you can't energise others.

AUTONOMY

L **ast,** but certainly not least, is autonomy: giving people more freedom. The more freedom people have over where, how and when they work, the happier and more productive they are. We have highlighted the importance of the commitment dividend or discretionary effort, and it is important to recognise that discretionary effort goes hand in hand with discretion and with freedom. There are a number of dimensions in which autonomy really counts: in terms of how the job is done, what the job consists of and where the work is done. There are, needless to say, serious restrictions in how far some staff can be given flexibility – and, indeed, in how much they want. But as a general principle, far greater autonomy over both task and time could be granted to the majority of employees.

We are particularly interested in working hours. Rather than the slightly depressing phrase 'work/life balance' (which is based on three flawed assumptions: life is good, work is bad and they're divisible), or the technocratic term 'flexible working', we advocate *time sovereignty*. The key is that individuals have the maximum degree of control over their time.

Does your employment contract state a specific number of hours you should work? Do you know what the number is? If so, do you work them? Quite. We all know that an arbitrary number of hours 'worked' – and especially 'worked' in the office – is a terrible measure of somebody's effectiveness. A wry smile or a wink often accompanies the phrase 'working from home', on the grounds that it is code for 'not working at all'. The opposite is true. People working from home are more productive than those in the office. When BT introduced home-working options, output rose by 20% in the piloted departments. To some extent, the better work rate could be the result of fewer distractions, but in a 2007 survey, two-thirds of those who work from home said that they put in the extra effort to demonstrate that they were, in fact, working.

Meanwhile, those who 'go to work' feel, at some level, as if they've done their bit simply by showing up. They have physically removed themselves from their own home to the office, sometimes at the cost of a really gruelling commute, recovery from which requires at least two cups of coffee. Eight hours later and it's time to go again, having achieved almost nothing, but feeling guilt-free because they showed up, they were there all day. There are still some organisations that manage people like that. It's a bit like managing a nursery class. 'Knell?' 'Yes, Miss.' (Tick present). 'Reeves?' 'Yes, Miss.' (Tick present.)

Technology means that physical presence is an even less useful proxy for productivity. We all know that technology allows us to work when we're not at work – BlackBerries, iPhones and wi-fi enabled laptops keep us constantly in touch, able to work all the time and anytime. (This means, of course, that time sovereignty really does have to mean sovereignty: you must use the awesome power of the 'off' button on those occasions when you want to stop working.)

But it is important to consider the other side of the coin: technology also allows us *not* to work when we *are* 'at work'. There's a wonderful chapter in *Dilbert: The Joy of Work*, by Scott Adams, headed 'Reverse Telecommuting'. The office has now become the ideal place to keep in touch with your friends, buy a lamp on eBay, update your insurance policy or find a holiday – but, thanks to our friend the computer, it looks exactly like work. For years, smart skivers have clocked on religiously, poured themselves a coffee and got on with some important life-management tasks. They might use a piece of software called a 'BossKey' to flip their PC instantly back to a screen of dull-looking work tasks should their manager happen to swing by for a chat. Ghostzilla and Ghostfox are versions of the browsing programmes Mozilla and Firefox with a tiny desktop icon which can be buried in another application, such as an e-mail or spreadsheet. If you don't know about these it means you are a) old, b) a boss, or c) both.

The point is not – repeat, not – that you should start clamping down on this sort of thing, introduce spy software, or institute rules about how many minutes each day employees are 'permitted' to use the internet for 'personal use'. For one thing, it won't work. For another, it's dumb. Within sensible constraints about the nature of content – most obviously with regard to inappropriate or illegal images – you should let people spend all day Googling a holiday or instant messaging their mates. It doesn't matter. The only thing that matters is whether they get their job done, not where and when they do so. If an employee fails to deliver, your performance-management systems will pick it up and you can fire them on the perfectly reasonable grounds that they are not doing their job.

If your performance-management system will not, in fact, pick up the fact that someone is not doing their job, we humbly submit that it is your performance-management system you really need to look at, not your policies on working hours or personal internet use.

SET YOUR PEOPLE FREE

If you set people free and simply trust them to do their job, we offer two guarantees. First, some people will abuse your trust. They will use their time sovereignty to avoid work altogether, or to do as little as humanly possible to prevent getting fired. Second, that it will be worth it anyway. Those who abuse a freer system are the same people who are abusing your current system by turning up on the dot of nine, leaving on the dot of five and doing nothing other than the bare minimum in the meantime. But the returns the organisation will get from the remainder, in terms of trust, motivation and engagement and productivity, will more than compensate for any of these losses. Time sovereignty does require a high degree of trust – and it is not only bosses who are sceptical. In the home-working survey quoted earlier, 60% thought that their co-workers would do less at home, and a quarter thought they would do nothing at all. The disease of presenteeism is not confined to the management classes, but it is managers and leaders who need to cure themselves of it most urgently.

You may have a nagging feeling that solidarity and autonomy rest uneasily together. If everyone is self-governing, free-wheeling around and working from home, how can they be part of a united team? We confess to the same anxiety. There is a tension here. But the rise in home-working is being driven by people who work from home for a day or two a week, rather than all of the time. The need and desire to be in the office, with colleagues, are unalterable facts of organisational life. Skype and e-mail are powerful tools. They are necessary – but not sufficient. They cannot support the building of communities of purpose, or the generation of organisational energy. But it's equally clear that great teams do not need to be together all of the time: world-class sports teams might train together two or three days a week at most. It is obviously a good idea to have some times of the week when the team tries to be together – rather like the market days of old. Beyond this, set your people free.

If you succeed in creating a solidaristic, energetic and autonomous culture, you will ensure higher levels of job satisfaction among your staff or team – and therefore a happier, more trusting and engaged workforce. But this is not your only measure of success. This kind of culture will also promote innovation, extra effort and higher productivity. Cold, hard cash: the subject of our next chapter.

CASH

When I asked my accountant if anything
could get me out of this mess I am in now
he thought for a long time and said,
'Yes, death would help.'

Robert Morley

If God only gave me a clear sign;
like making a large deposit in my
name at a Swiss bank.

Woody Allen

JUST WHAT IS ACCOUNTING ANYWAY?

It's often asserted that accounting is the language of business.[1] The conduct of business is certainly unimaginable without it. At its broadest, accounting has been defined by the American Accounting Association as 'The process of identifying, measuring, and communicating economic information to permit informed judgements and decisions by users of the information.'

There – that's got you interested. It's a good job accountants don't run the sales and marketing department. An equally accurate definition of accounting might be: 'You will never consistently make money, control your costs, make the best use of your resources, or be able to decide where to focus your efforts inside your business unless you understand the fundamental rules of accounting.'

If you're going to run any enterprise, you have to understand the language of accounts. Fortunately, you can make sense of accounts with a comparatively limited vocabulary. To set you on your way, we have provided a glossary of financial terms at the end of this chapter.

AN ANCIENT ART

The power and relevance of accounting is underscored by the longevity of its central tenets – some of the basic rules of accounting haven't changed since Ancient Rome. Let us introduce you to the real Godfather.

Luca Pacioli (1445–1517) was a Franciscan friar who produced the first printed description of the double entry accounting system in 1494, in order to 'give the trader without delay information as to his assets and liabilities'.[2] We hope Luca would smile on our efforts to summarise the key foundations of accounting.

THE FOUR GOLDEN RULES

Accounting is fundamentally a rule-based discipline. A fully fledged MBA accounting model would equip you with a plethora of rules, on both the practice of accounting and on widely accepted public standards of reporting financial information. Our ambition here is much more limited: to provide you with the four key tenets of financial accounting that will gift you the necessary financial literacy to understand a set of basic accounts.

What are they?

- A DOUBLE ENTRY SYSTEM INVOLVES RECORDING THE EFFECTS OF EACH TRANSACTION AS DEBITS AND CREDITS
- LEFT-HAND SIDE OF AN ACCOUNT IS THE DEBIT SIDE, AND THE RIGHT-HAND SIDE IS THE CREDIT SIDE
- TOTAL DEBITS MUST EQUAL TOTAL CREDITS
- THE ACCOUNTING EQUATION: ASSETS = LIABILITIES + CAPITAL

The problem, of course, is remembering these rules – until now that is.

GOLDEN RULE 1: A DOUBLE ENTRY SYSTEM INVOLVES RECORDING THE EFFECTS OF EACH TRANSACTION AS DEBITS AND CREDITS

The cornerstone of the double entry system is that each transaction is recorded with at least one debit and one credit.

This is because each party in a business transaction will receive something and give something in return. In book-keeping terms, what is received is a debit (something comes 'IN' when looking at the entry of a debit item) and what is given is a credit (something is going 'OUT' when looking at the entry of a credit item).

This should alert you to the vital fact that the words *credit* and *debit* have a very specific meaning in accounting, different from their use in everyday language.

So, for example, let's say that *The 80 Minute MBA* company pays cash to buy a photocopier for £500. How would this transaction be recorded as a debit and a credit? As the table below shows, if we think of a debit as something coming 'IN' there would be a debit entry in the Machinery account, and if we think of a credit as something going 'OUT' there would be a credit entry in the Cash account.

EFFECT	BOOK-KEEPING ACTION
Photocopier comes IN	A *debit* entry in the Machinery account
Cash goes OUT	A *credit* entry in the Cash account

GOLDEN RULE 2: THE LEFT-HAND SIDE OF AN ACCOUNT IS THE DEBIT SIDE, AND THE RIGHT-HAND SIDE IS THE CREDIT SIDE

If every transaction creates a debit and a credit, how do we record them in our accounts? Which is where Golden Rule 2 comes in – namely that the left-hand side of an account is always the debit side and the right-hand side of the account is always the credit side.

In its simplest form, an account consists of three parts:

- **THE TITLE OF THE ACCOUNT (ITS NAME)**
- **A LEFT OR DEBIT SIDE**
- **A RIGHT OR CREDIT SIDE**

Because the alignment of these parts of an account resembles the letter T, it is referred to as a T account.

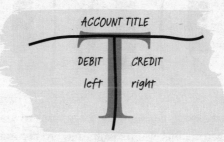

You will also sometimes see T accounts depicted to represent a scale or balance. If this feels a new or unfamiliar rule, think of your bank statements – your current account statements – which adopt the same convention of debits on the left and credits on the right.

And the overall accounts of a business are, in simple terms, the amalgam of a wide range of different T accounts which feature in any business, such as assets, liabilities and capital.

Part of the *hard yards* in accounting is remembering how different types of transactions are recorded in different T accounts. Again, clear rules apply and are summarised in the diagram below, which features in any standard accounting textbook. All asset accounts are increased with debits and decreased with credits. Liabilities and capital work in the opposite way to assets.

Rules for Double Entry

Before we leave Golden Rule 2 we want to make sure you're getting this. Think debits and credits – now shut your eyes. Were you seeing them automatically on the left and right – debits left, credits right? If not, we have a simple suggestion to help you remember.

Look at the letters below.

AC ⚡ DC

When we think of AC/DC we think of Angus Young, Gibson SG guitars and the best rock and roll band ever. If you didn't, perhaps you thought power supply instead. Either way – although we prefer the rock reference – think whichever you choose, but think AC/DC. Look at the order of the words.

Think every account (AC) comprises of debits and credits (DC).

Think DC: debits come before credits.

Think DC: the D is on the left, the C is on the right.
Debits on the left, credits on the right.

Think debits and credits – shut your eyes and try again.

$$AC \,\lightning\, DC$$

Account (entries) must be / Debits (left) and Credits (right)

GOLDEN RULE 3: TOTAL DEBITS MUST EQUAL TOTAL CREDITS

If you can remember our earlier diagram of a T account shown as a balance scale, you should never forget Golden Rule 3: that after every transaction is recorded in the company accounts, total debits must equal total credits.

Back to our recently purchased *The 80 Minute MBA* photocopier – which was paid for in cash, at a cost of £500 – our book-keeping entry would read:

ACCOUNT	DEBIT	CREDIT
Machinery	£500	£0
Cash	£0	£500

In this example, the books stay in balance because the exact pounds sterling amount that increase the value of our Machinery account decreases the value of our Cash account.

GOLDEN RULE 4: THE ACCOUNTING EQUATION

Thus far we have seen that every transaction must be recorded once on the debit side of an account and once on the credit side of an account, and that total debits must equal total credits.

In this way, double entry booking follows the strictures of our final golden rule – the accounting equation[3] – which states that:

Assets = liabilities + capital

It is a mathematical equation and the equals sign (=) requires that both sides of the equation stay in balance at all times. In other words, the equation must be in balance after every recorded transaction in the system.

What does the accounting equation mean in simple terms? Namely that the economic resources of a business (the assets) must be equal to the claims on those economic resources (liabilities + capital). What you have should be equal to what you owe.

Assets consist of property of all kinds, such as buildings, machinery and stocks of goods. Other assets include debts owed by customers and the amount of money in the bank account. Liabilities include amounts owed by the business for goods and services supplied to the business and for expenses incurred by the businesses that have not yet been paid for. They also include funds borrowed by the business. Capital is often called the owner's equity. It comprises the funds invested in the business by the owner plus any profits retained for use in the business less any share of the profits paid out of the business to the owner.[4]

So back to the idea of an entity as made up of resources and claims on those resources. A good way to think of the accounting equation is captured in the diagram below.

Business misery results when the claims on an entity's resources continually outstrip its resources.

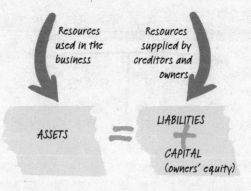

Resources used in the business

Resources supplied by creditors and owners

ASSETS = LIABILITIES + CAPITAL (owners' equity)

FROM EQUATIONS TO T ACCOUNTS TO BALANCE SHEETS

Whilst you may not have heard about the accounting equation before, you will undoubtedly have heard about a balance sheet before, which is simply the accounting equation expressed in a financial statement.

The balance sheet documents the accounting equation at a particular point in time. As the name implies, and as determined by the accounting equation, *it has to balance* – i.e. the value of the assets must be equal to the claims made against those assets.

When one looks at a balance sheet, you can see our four golden rules threaded through it, with debits on the left, credits on the right and the need for balance.

The link between the accounting equation and normal T accounts is a simple one. Debits are positive numbers that are represented on the left side of the accounting equation, and credits are positive numbers represented on the right side of the accounting equation.

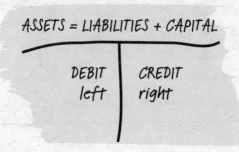

ASSETS = LIABILITIES + CAPITAL

| DEBIT | CREDIT |
| left | right |

The same financial and spatial relationships are replicated in the presentation of a balance sheet, as our example below shows. Happily, *The 80 Minute MBA* is as yet a simple business.

'THE 80 MINUTE MBA' BALANCE SHEET AT THE END OF PERIOD 1

ASSETS		LIABILITIES	
Cash at bank	£1,000	Accounts payable	£1,000
Accounts receivable	£1,000		
Photocopier	£500	Total liabilities:	£1,000
		CAPITAL	
		John Knell	£750
		Richard Reeves	£750
		Total capital:	£1,500
Total:	£2,500		
		Total:	£2,500

Who said understanding accounts was complicated? Just remember our four golden rules. Or, more simply, remember:

AC ⚡ DC

And remember that what you have should be equal to what you owe. For those about to balance, we salute you.

FINANCIAL ACCOUNTING GLOSSARY

Assets: an asset is something a company *owns* which has future economic value (land, buildings, equipment, goodwill etc.).

Liability: a liability is something a company *owes* (money, service, product etc.).

Revenues: amounts received or to be received from customers for sales of products or services (sales, rent or interest).

Capital: often called the owner's equity. It comprises the funds invested in the business by the owner and what's left of the assets after liabilities have been deducted.

Profit: revenue less costs.

The profit and loss account: summarises a business's trading transactions – income, sales and expenditure – and the resulting profit or loss for a given period.

A balance sheet: provides a financial snapshot at a given point in time listing all of the assets and liabilities of a company.

A balance sheet shows:
- Fixed assets – long-term possessions.
- Current assets – short-term possessions.
- Current liabilities – what the business owes and must repay in the short term.
- Long-term liabilities – including owner's or shareholders' capital.

The balance sheet is so called because there is a debit entry and credit entry for everything, which must balance.

The balance sheet shows:
- How solvent the business is.
- How liquid its assets are – how much is in the form of cash or can easily be converted into cash, i.e. stocks and shares.

- How the business is financed.
- How much capital is being used.

These definitions are drawn in large part from www.businesslink.gov.uk and supplemented by some material from Woods, F. and Robinson, S. (2004) *Book-Keeping and Accounting*, FT Prentice Hall.

RESOURCES
SUPPLY CHAIN MANAGEMENT

Certain management disciplines have slowly become the new rock and roll of business efficiency and delivery. If project management is one, the undisputed king of business integration is supply chain management.

The supermarket sector and car manufacturers are the most commonly cited examples of sophisticated and integrated supply chains where technology has enabled end-customers requirements to be communicated directly to suppliers, enabling both greater customisation of supply and lower levels of standing inventory inside supplying businesses.

But how do we define a supply chain? The supply chain is normally understood to extend from the raw material or extraction through many processes to the ultimate sale or delivery to the final consumer, whether goods or services. Arguably, it can also include the disposal of the waste associated with the consumed product.[5]

Recent developments have ensured that supply chain management has become a vital source of strategic and tactical value to businesses. The affordances of IT have created new opportunities for close cooperation between suppliers and key customers, whilst concerns about sustainability and other associated ethical demands on the supply chain are forcing producers to develop highly transparent and resource-sensitive supply chains.

So supply chains matter to consumers and producers – even if they don't excite the average MBA student.

Here's a fairly typical diagram of a supply chain matrix:

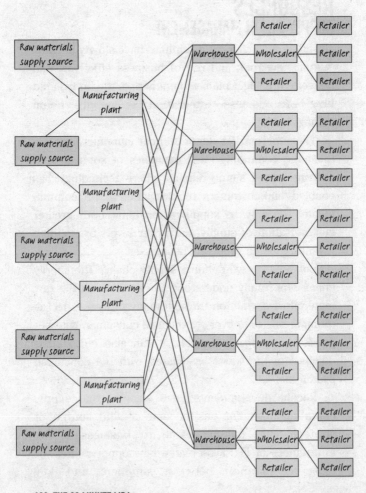

We're going spend a little time now explaining how you, and your business, can best secure the full benefits that exemplary supply chain management can bring.

So what's the main thing you need to do?

Hire someone who really understands the diagram opposite!

INSTANT ECONOMICS

People who have studied economics tend to be quite a self-satisfied bunch. Fair enough: it's a difficult, technical subject. They look upon those unacquainted with the core concepts of the dismal science with a mixture of pity and contempt. Given the limits on your time, a three-year degree in economics followed by a doctorate in econometric modelling is probably not on the cards. But the killer line which economists often use is 'Well, can you at least draw supply and demand curves?' Any MBA worth their salt must be able to meet this challenge and dash off the basic supply and demand model on the back of a napkin, or on a newspaper in the back of a cab.

DEMAND

Demand is an expression of how much people want something, measured in terms of how much they're willing to pay for it – or, to put it slightly differently, how much of it they'll buy at a certain price. So here's how a demand curve for, say, widgets might look.

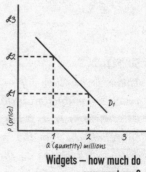

Widgets – how much do you want one?

You may notice that the 'curve' is, in fact, a straight line. This is a trick to try to catch out non-economists – always call it a curve. Price (P) is measured on the vertical axis, and quantity (Q) on the horizontal one. (We remember the order by thinking of the phrase 'Mind your Ps and Qs', but we're pretty sure we are alone in this.) D_1 is the demand line – yes, very good, the curve *– and represents a given level of demand for the widgets in question. At this level of demand (D_1), consumers will buy two million widgets for £1, or one million for £2. Demand is rarely static, however, and of course the goal of the widget supplier's marketing department is to raise the level of demand so that people will pay*

more for the widgets or buy more at the same price. If widgets become all the rage, the demand curve will shift upwards. At this higher level of demand (D_2), consumers will buy two million widgets with a price tag of £2 and buy a million even if the price rises to £3:

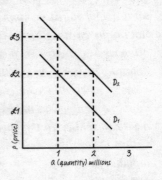

Widgets – the new 'must have' item

SUPPLY

There is another factor influencing the price: how much the widget manufacturer has to charge per item to cover their costs and produce a reasonable profit for shareholders. So the supply curve, going in the opposite direction to the demand curve, shows how many widgets will be supplied at any given price:

In this case, a million widgets will be supplied at a price of £1.50 per unit, and two million widgets will be supplied if the price is £2.50. Of course, supply curves can move too, especially in response to a change in the price of raw materials.

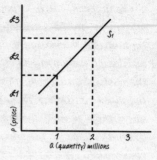

Widget supply lines

EQUILIBRIUM

Once the demand and supply curves for widgets are known, both the prevailing price charged and the quantity supplied will be established by the 'equilibrium' point between demand and supply: in other words, the place where the lines cross. In this case (assuming demand at D₁), the answer is that 1.25 million widgets will be sold at a price of £1.75.

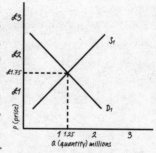

Widgets — how many for how much?

But...

Of course, it's much more complicated than this. The textbook models assume perfect information and perfect rationality. In truth, markets are driven by human emotions like greed, fear and hope. If 2008 taught us anything, it taught us this. And don't make the mistake of confusing price and value. The model gives you the price, but not necessarily the true value.

Gold is very, very expensive. Water is cheap. But which is more valuable? Finally, remember that economists never agree with each other and are just as likely to be wrong as right. (Sometimes they console themselves by saying that they were wrong, but 'for the right reasons'.) They often see both sides of every question – which is why the US President Harry S. Truman once demanded: 'Bring me a one-armed economist.' He was fed up with economists answering his questions with a variation of 'Well, on the one hand X, but on the other hand Y.'

CONVER-
SATION

Marketers concern themselves with acquiring and retaining customers, who are the lifeblood of an organization. They attract customers by learning about potential needs, helping to develop products that customers want, creating awareness, and communicating benefits; they retain them by ensuring that they get good value, appropriate service, and a stream of future products.

Harvard Business School

The problem with the world today is communication. Too much communication.

Homer Simpson

THE RISE AND RISE OF THE PRODUCING CONSUMER

In our experience, the best marketers do not lack bravado. But even they are struggling to project steely self-confidence in the face of profound changes to the world in which they do business.

One of the most visible manifestations of these changes will already be familiar to you – the rise of new media and the challenge to the supremacy of traditional TV and print advertising. If you have a Sky+ box or Virgin Media's V+ service, you will already be watching more TV on demand and time-shifting your media consumption.[1] Or maybe you are increasingly using your mobile phone or laptop to download viewable content on demand, perhaps using the BBC's iPlayer or other similar services. What you may not have noticed is that you will also be watching less TV advertising.

This fragmentation of the old broadcast model as a route to consumers – the so-called *one-to-many* model of communication – represents the silting up of one of marketing's main channels of communication. But what is replacing it – the rise of so-called *many-to-many*

communications – heralds a seismic shift in the power and predilections of consumers and is, of course, a much more significant challenge to marketing practice.

The internet and new forms of social software[2] and social media, such as blogs and social network services, are affording consumers the ability to contribute as well as receive information. Good examples of where such interactions are taking place include Dell's IdeaStorm, Facebook, flickr, Linkedin and bebo. Everyone used to be a viewer, reader or listener. But now everyone can also be a broadcaster and content provider. Thus we have moved from the world of *one-to-many* to *many-to-many* communications.

These new weapons of mass collaboration[3] allow thousands upon thousands of individuals and communities to create content,[4] share ideas and interests, talk to each other, talk to you, leave recommendations, share networks and causes and build or break brand reputations. We are no longer passive consumers, but are becoming active producers.

For some, this shift heralds a genuinely new epoch – the age of mass innovation,[5] in which we are democratising the production and consumption of everything as we change the way we communicate and share. All of this is having a decisive impact on how companies talk to their markets, and on the very nature of markets themselves.

As a consequence, marketing experts have been quick to proclaim the slow death of cold-calling or the 30-second advertising slot,[6] as the relative disconnect between marketer (sender) and consumer (receiver) is widening.[7]

The argument runs that *old marketing* – 'the act of interrupting masses of people with ads about average products' – is being replaced by *new marketing* – 'which leverages scarce attention and creates interactions among communities with similar interests'.[8]

Enterprises are having to come to terms with the real fear that more and more of their increasingly fickle and media-sophisticated consumer base are turning away from them and their message.

FROM MARKETING TO CONVERSATION

What does all this mean for how businesses reach and influence their customers? In simple terms, the outcome is that companies, products and markets, and the communities that sustain them, are increasingly built by conversation. If marketing was once the essential differentiator in ensuring that a new product or service met consumer need, it is being usurped by a less controlled and more dynamic interaction between producer and consumer. For all sorts of enterprises, the ability to create new ideas, products and opportunities is becoming rooted in their ability to stage new conversations with their markets and their customers. And why is conversation such a powerful word to capture all this? Because it is an inherently creative activity. As Theodore Zeldin has memorably said, 'When minds meet, they don't just exchange facts; they transform them, reshape them, draw different implications from them, engage in new trains of thought. Conversation does not simply reshuffle the cards. It creates new cards.'[9]

The challenge for marketing is that its core instinct is to attempt to influence the customer in a *controlled* way. This is precisely the opposite of what is now required for success, which is a more dynamic and messy flow of information, ideas and exchange between producer and consumer in which both parties will change their approach or perception as a result.

FROM THE FOUR Ps TO THE FOUR Cs

If the aim of marketing is to satisfy customer needs or wants, how has the discipline traditionally approached this challenge?

The dominant conceptual model underpinning marketing strategy has been the so-called *marketing mix* – which is a generalised model used to describe the different kinds of choices organisations have to make in the whole process of bringing a product or service to market.

The most famous shorthand for those broad choices remains the Four Ps framework, originally proposed by E. Jerome McCarthy, focusing on product, price, place and promotion, which taken together provide the basic components of a marketing plan.[10]

The first two Ps (product and price) are in essence product-related elements. The other two Ps are parts of the delivery system – with 'place' about delivering the physical product or service and 'promotion' about delivering the 'sales messages' and communicating with potential customers.[11]

Different products will produce different points of emphasis, or balance, within the marketing mix. So, for example, within industrial markets more emphasis is usually given to direct contact (involving face-to-face selling), as opposed to the indirect techniques (of marketing research and advertising) used in most consumer markets.[12]

The recent history of marketing has been driven by the partial rejection and ongoing modification of the basic Four Ps model. Marketers have busily been adding extra Ps to the model – like throwing bricks on a failing coastal defence as the tide creeps ever higher.[13] The additional Ps, such as 'people' and 'process', have been added to ensure the model is equally applicable to services as well as product markets.

But the demise of the Four Ps model is a metaphor for the broader collapse of marketing certainties. The challenge is no longer to adapt existing models, but to accept that the rules of the game have changed – and as a consequence so must the very essence of marketing.

The Four Ps are being taken over by the Four Cs:

- COMMUNITY
- CO-CREATION
- CUSTOMISATION
- CONVERSATION

COMMUNITY – FRIEND OR FOE?

The first big challenge for traditional marketing is that success is no longer just about enlisting individual consumers any more, but about how best to engage the communities in which they hang out, hunt and harangue.

Consumption, it appears, really is best served in a crowd.[14]

The problem for companies is that as consumers have become more valuable, they have also become more vengeful. Both these attributes demand that enterprises should seek to be in constant conversation with them.

Some of those conversations are with individuals who are their biggest friends and fans – they're people who love them already. The challenge then is how to amplify their contribution and voice.

But some are with their biggest foes. They've been burned by a bad product or poor customer service and they're intent on flaming the reputation of the offending company. Enterprises must work even harder to stay in the conversation game with them, but to a different end – to get them to change their pitch or their tone or, better still, to get them to talk about something else altogether.

Let's look at some examples, starting with community as foe.

Some of you may be familiar with the very large motor vehicles produced by the Hummer company. Whilst designed largely for off-road pursuits, they are unfortunately normally found very much on-road, partially blocking a side street near you. Buying one is not a good leadership decision – unless you're fighting in the desert. Many people in London live in flats smaller than Hummers and going to the local shops in a Hummer is a bit like taking a bath in full diving gear – you look ridiculous and it adds nothing to the experience.

Perhaps unsurprisingly, this in-your-face product has produced an in-your-face response from consumers, the most provocative of which is the ihumpedyourhummer website (www.ihumpedyour-hummer.com).[15]

The site's founders began the initiative as a protest against the various ways they think Hummers deface benign public spaces. The group's manifesto welcomes 'all who peacefully and articulately challenge the legitimacy of the Hummer today, whether their motivations be politically, environmentally, or otherwise informed'. Over time, the site has turned into something decidedly strange rather than articulate.

Perhaps the site's name undercut any nobler intention the founders may have had and it now does exactly what it says on the tin, affording the opportunity for individuals to go and deface Hummers in a way analogous to 'humping' and posting those videos on the site and almost always on YouTube, where a wide variety of 'Hummer humping' videos are available for your delectation.

Not a particularly enjoyable post-coital conversation for Hummer. Although, looking on the bright side, they should perhaps be arguing that no car can withstand a good humping quite like a Hummer.

Another notable consumer-led campaign has been against PayPal, the company which provides secure ways to send and receive money online (www.paypal.com). A group of campaigners accused PayPal of fashioning their terms of service, which you must sign if you want to use PayPal, in such a way that it encourages consumers to waive their rights under credit card consumer protection laws. They have set up the PayPal Sucks site (www.paypalsucks.com) to publicise their allegations and others have posted critical reports of the company's customer service. Whatever the merits of their allegations – and we personally do not think that PayPal Sucks – that's not really the point. The point is that PayPal have experienced a 'community' problem.

The power of this example is that it could, of course, be *www.AnyCompanySucks.com* because that's a conversation that most large enterprises will at some stage inevitably find themselves engaged in. The key skill when they do is knowing when to cut their losses and change tack as a result.

For example, in 2007 HSBC were forced into a major U-turn on their initial decision to charge graduating students 9.9% APR on their overdrafts. A student campaign was set up on Facebook to coordinate opposition against the charges – called, rather succinctly, 'Stop the Great HSBC Graduate Rip-Off' – which attracted nearly 5,000 members and was absolutely pivotal in forcing HSBC to think again about their proposals.

In response to the campaign, HSBC took the decision to freeze interest charging on 2007 graduate overdrafts up to £1,500. In their press release, HSBC bank said that it was not too big to listen to its customers.[16]

These are sobering examples for marketers – and might tempt you to agree with Seth Godin's recent warning that '…you're not in charge. And your prospects don't care about you.'[17]

But the redeeming feature of consumers is that they can also be a company's greatest friends – and the best companies have a natural instinct to enlist and animate their fans. The most successful modern brands have given rise to the fandom phenomenon – legions of fans that wait eagerly for any new product issue or news. Fans of Apple Mac computers really are happy to be called 'Macolytes'[18] and at best act as powerful brand evangelists, blogging, reviewing and proselytising about Apple's new offerings to market.

But enhanced word-of-mouth marketing is only one benefit from getting the conversation right with your consumers. The biggest prize of all awaits those companies who can turn them into *prosumers* – consumers who help create the products and services they themselves want to use.[19] This is the vision of consumer as producer and co-creator.

Any idea what this is?

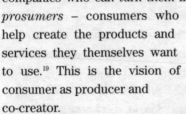

It's a MINDSTORMS® robot made by LEGO® Group.

When the product first made its debut in 1989, LEGO® Group's marketers were surprised to discover that the robotic toys were popular not only with teenagers, the envisaged market, but also with adult hobbyists eager to improve them.

Adult hobbyists. That's a descriptive phrase to conjure with. We mean geeks – people who live with their heads inside computers, wearing slogan t-shirts, looking longingly at screens, and creating unimaginative profiles (they're geeks, remember) on internet dating sites. But they're a market – and a much more lucrative market than LEGO® Group ever imagined.

Within weeks of releasing the product, MINDSTORMS® robot communities had sprung up who had hacked into the electronics, reprogrammed the robots and then began to send their suggested improvements to LEGO® Group.

LEGO® Group's response?

They threatened legal action – the conversational equivalent of a slamming door, only less eloquent.

As their consumers rebelled, with fans turning into foes, eventually LEGO® Group came round. It embraced the hacker community – about to become MINDSTORMS's® biggest fans and backers – and wrote a 'right to hack' into the MINDSTORMS® software licence, giving hobbyists explicit permission to let their imaginations run wild. Now, every time a customer posts a new application for MINDSTORMS®, the toy becomes more valuable.[20]

LEGO® Group thankfully moved from very dumb to smart just in time. If you recognise that customers have more power than ever before and that you're now in the conversation business, so can you. And you shouldn't give up hope that you might still be able to read their minds.

NEUROMARKETING

*The influential British economist Lionel Robbins declared that it was not possible to 'peer into men's minds' to discover their true desires. But that was three-quarters of a century ago. Now we are peering in earnest. A fast-growing sub-discipline of neurology and marketing, **neuromarketing**, represents a terrifically exciting scientific advance into the understanding of consumer behaviour – or a totally terrifying Orwellian development, depending on your point of view. The word itself was coined in 2002, but the discipline has only recently begun to take off.*

Subjects are placed in MRI scanners while they look at images, or attached to mobile brain-imaging machines while they shop. Then neuro-scientists can see what happens to their brains when they buy something, see a brand name they recognise, or swallow a mouth-ful of a soft drink. The most famous example is a high-tech version of the 'Coke versus Pepsi' challenge. The findings from

Samuel McClure and his colleagues were startling. When people did not know what they were drinking, roughly half said they preferred each brand. The subjects' ventromedial prefrontal cortex – essentially the brain's feel-good centre – was actually more strongly activated by Pepsi than Coke.

But when the guinea pigs knew what they were drinking, the scans revealed activity in the hippocampus, midbrain and dorsolateral prefrontal cortex: areas associated with memory and feelings.

Here is what the researchers concluded: 'Subjects in this part of the experiment preferred Coke in the labelled cups significantly more than Coke in the anonymous tasks... We hypothesize that cultural information biases preference decisions through the dorsolateral region of the prefrontal cortex, with the hippocampus engaged to recall the associated information.' To you and me: such is the power of Coke's brand that people do not merely think *they prefer it to Pepsi. They actually* do *prefer it, so long as they know what they're drinking. Scary stuff.*[21]

CUSTOMISATION

The idea of customer-driven customisation is hardly a new one. Motor manufacturers have for many decades offered consumers a bewildering array of options on any new car they might order, with automated manufacturing systems enabling the manufacturer to reduce the lead times on any customised order and maintain a competitive price.

But the internet and other interactive technologies have greatly expanded the possibilities for customisation, popularising the idea of mass customisation in which the personalisation of products and services for individual customers is no longer the preserve of the wealthy, but is deliverable to all customers at a price point equivalent to traditionally mass-produced goods.[22]

One interesting aspect of this experience for the consumer is that nearly all of us have become auxiliary workers for many of the service providers we most frequently do business with. When was the last time you spoke to a bank employee or a travel agent? Increasingly, we book and manage our finances online, and specify and book our travel arrangements and itineraries. We are prepared to put in a little extra time for the convenience of customisation and for the comfort of control.

The power of this shift can be seen in how much the language of service providers has completely changed in recent years, across both the public and private sectors. The National Health Service now talks about offering patients personalised care, in which people should have more choice about when they are able to see their GP and over their treatment and care. As the Health Secretary commented in early 2008: 'The days of patients being the passive recipients of one-size-fits-all service are over.'[23]

It would appear that you can now have any service you like, as long as it is personalised, customised and fitted to your exact requirements. Well, maybe. But the aspiration at least is becoming hard-wired into the expectations of both providers and consumer alike.

If consumers are being actively encouraged to tune into their inner preferences and give free rein to their choices, the internet is allowing markets to be restructured in ways that support our appetite for

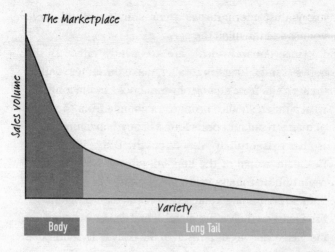

The Long Tail

customisation – with the outcome being the ever greater segmentation of particular markets and customer bases. As one expert notes, as a consequence, '…the mass market is turning into a market of niches'.[24]

This phenomenon has been brilliantly captured by Chris Anderson, in his *Long Tail* model.

As Anderson notes: 'The theory of the long tail can be boiled down to this: Our culture and economy are increasingly shifting away from a focus on a relatively small number of hits (mainstream products and markets) at the head of the demand curve, and moving toward a huge number of niches in the tail.'

In other words, the body of the long tail represents the hits, the bestsellers. The tail trailing behind represents the many products that reach niche markets of a few consumers. But when this long tail of mini-markets is added together, it is as large as the mass market of hits.

Thus producers and retailers can make significant profits by selling small volumes of hard-to-find items to many customers rather than simply selling large volumes of the hits.

Thus, Amazon, who are frequently cited as the quintessential long-tail retailer, make the largest part of their profits from selling obscure books in the long tail, with a much smaller proportion coming from the sales of mainstream hit books found in any bookstore.

The extraordinary success of the BBC's iPlayer is a further example of the long-tail effects, with the BBC reporting that many users are seeking out more niche interest programmes and, as a consequence, programmes broadcast on their more niche digital channels have seen increased viewing as a result of the iPlayer. By June 2008 iPlayer had approximately five million page views per day, and by December 2008 over 180 million programmes had been watched on iPlayer since release.[25]

So perhaps the simplest way to think about the long tail is as the story of 'how products that were once considered fringe, underground or independent now collectively make up a market that rivals the bestsellers and blockbusters'.[26]

The internet has been vital in enabling these long-tail business models to thrive, by simultaneously lowering the search costs of the consumer in finding niche content, increasing the population of available goods and dramatically lowering the costs of reaching consumers.[27]

And whilst internet businesses have dominated discussion of the long tail, digital technology is making it easy for consumers to customise non-digital goods. More esoteric examples include the proliferation of microbrews as the long tail of beer, the growth of customised t-shirts, shoes and other clothing as the long tail of fashion, and the growth of online universities as the long tail of education.[28]

All of this has had a juddering impact on marketing practice, with long-tail economics transforming what is marketable, what is saleable, what is interesting, and to whom.[29] The long tail means a long haul for marketers.

CO-CREATION

Standing on the shoulders of community and customisation is the other key disrupter to traditional marketing – co-creation.

Firms can no longer create value in splendid isolation. Value is increasingly being co-created by the firm and the consumer, as consumers actively help design, develop and distribute the products and services they value.

This scrambling of the value chain reflects the heightened desire of consumers to play with and shape the things they care about. But it also, rather paradoxically, makes innovation potentially more manageable.

The big risk in new product and service innovation for companies is to anticipate correctly how consumers will respond to and use their new market offerings. Consumer-driven innovation and co-creation diminishes these risks, as consumers actively design products and services to meet their wants and needs. Moreover, they often create new markets and sources of value as a consequence.[30]

An excellent example is the emergence of the mountain bike. The original examples of the mountain bike were garage-built by enthusiastic riders in California in the early 1970s. These consumer innovators created a market which slowly, but inevitably, commercial bike manufacturers responded to as they actively collaborated with these consumer producers. As Leadbeater has detailed, by 2004, mountain bikes and related equipment accounted for 65% of all bike sales in the US. 'A category has been invented by passionate users that was worth $58 billion dollars.'[31]

Perhaps the most powerful example of consumer co-creation is Wikipedia, which is now the largest encyclopaedia in the world. Its success is a story of how a simple piece of web software – coupled to an inspiring vision – has galvanised a global community of volunteers to help fashion one of the world's five most popular web properties. Part cause, part community, part collective, but totally co-created. The cause is an inspiring one. 'Imagine a world in which every single person on the planet is given free access to the sum of all human knowledge. That's our commitment.'[32]

Its realisation has been built upon web software called a wiki – which, to get into the spirit a little, Wikipedia tells us is the Hawaiian word for 'fast' and is sometimes expanded to 'what I know is'.

A wiki allows multiple users to create and edit the same web page. What is truly extraordinary about Wikipedia are the numbers of people who have done just that. Over the last eight years volunteers, dedicated to sharing knowledge freely and by their passion for particular topics, have contributed more than 11 million articles in 265 languages.[33] You mean you haven't uploaded an entry yet?

The scale of volunteer activity is such that, as of December 2008, Wikipedia, despite having just 23 paid staff and annual expenses of less than six million dollars, is attracting more than 275 million users to the site every month to access information, free of charge and free of advertising. That's a rough staff ratio of 11.95 million visitors per month per staff member.[33] Co-creation certainly does wonders for your productivity numbers.[34]

Of course, Wikipedia has its detractors, with the main gripe being that the site is full of inaccurate entries.

In this sense, Wikipedia is a live beta test of public peer review and the broader premise that collaboration among users will over time improve content, in the way that the open-source community steadily improved Linus Torvalds' first version of Linux.[36] This is in part what makes it such an interesting product – it is, in effect, self-repairing, fluid and free.

Marketers are only beginning to come to terms with what co-creation is going to mean for marketing strategy and practice. Expect numerous 'how to' books on how to market in a community environment without alienating consumers. *Giving Up Control To Regain It* is likely to be one of the titles.

What is already clear is that marketers are not going to be able to ignore Wikipedia, with recent research from the US suggesting that four out of ten consumers consider Wikipedia very influential in online purchasing decisions.[37]

Perhaps unsurprisingly, the blogs of new marketing experts are already suggesting that Wikipedia entries related to product categories (remember, Wikipedia is free of advertising) are fair game for direct influence by marketing directors. As one marketer notes, why wouldn't the marketing director of Vitamins Inc seek to make expert entries into a Wikipedia page on ginseng or other vitamins in their product ranges?[38]

Celebrate co-creation and keep using Wikipedia, but stay curious and sceptical about entries – and let's hope public peer review can muzzle marketers on the make as effectively as any other interest group.

CONVERSATION

The final C is, of course, conversation. Marketers have long claimed that they are the generator of the customer eye view of any business, stressing that their overriding mission is to engage with their customers as much as possible in as many different ways as possible.

Maybe – marketers have never lacked a sales pitch, after all. But those companies clinging to the certainties of old marketing models won't deliver on this mission. The Four Cs are rapidly undermining the core of almost all traditional marketing theory. Community, customisation and co-creation are eroding the gap between marketing on one side, and the customer on the other.

As one expert puts it: 'It's not us and them. It's us and us.'[39]

Marketers need to accept that their consumers are taking more critical marketing decisions than their marketing departments.[40] This means that marketing practice must become rooted in dialogue, partnership and co-creation with the consumer, as the age of tightly controlled communication and connection fades.

And most companies need to accept that they urgently need elocution lessons.

As Christopher Locke and his colleagues note: 'Most corporations... only know how to talk in the soothing, humourless monotone of the mission statement, marketing brochure, and your-call-is-important-to-us busy signal. Same old tone, same old lies. No wonder networked markets have no respect for companies unable or unwilling to speak as they do.'[41]

Consumers have changed. Marketers are going to have to change with them – and learn the art of conversation.

THANK YOU FOR YOUR 80 MINUTES.

GENERAL RESOURCES

We hope that this book makes you more business curious – not just in terms of searching out the key texts and references that we direct you to in each of our individual chapter resources and references sections, but also in terms of how best to make use of a wide range of additional print and online materials.

EDITED BOOKS AND COLLECTIONS

A number of the key business schools produce excellent summary series covering key business and management issues. See for example the *Harvard Business Review* Paperback series, which features highly readable collections of seminal essays from the *Harvard Business Review* (*HBR*) grouped by theme – such as marketing, leadership and corporate social responsibility (www.hbsp.harvard.edu).

LEADING BUSINESS SCHOOLS IN THE UK AND GLOBALLY

Almost all of the leading business schools now provide freely downloadable podcasts or other audio visual media, featuring lectures by their main teaching faculty or other guest expert speakers. The podcasts cover both key elements of an MBA syllabus and also key topical issues – most notably in the last 12 months, the current financial crisis.

For example, London Business School's podcast page (www.london.edu/podcast.html) features lectures on a wide range of subjects, including why marketing is so important, macroeconomics, social networks and closing the gap between strategy and execution.

In a similar vein, since 2001, Massachusetts Institute of Technology (MIT) has produced almost 600 hours of lectures, which are available for free from the MIT World website (www.mitworld.mit/edu), with content searchable by theme and speaker.

More broadly, a wide range of leading universities from around the globe are now using the iTunes platform, specifically the iTunes University (www.apple.com/itunesu), to distribute podcasts of expert lecture and teaching materials. Apple are effectively creating a global lecture theatre for the engaged *80 Minute MBA* student.

The UK-based Open University released more than 300 lectures as iTunes University courses in June 2008, and Oxford University and the Wharton School at the University of Pennsylvania have also followed suit. At the time of going to press, the top three Oxford University downloads on the iTunes University were Joseph Stiglitz on the credit crunch, a range of lectures exploring J. R. R. Tolkien's relationship with Oxford University and the John Locke lectures in Philosophy.

If *The 80 Minute MBA* encourages you to pursue just one of those sets of lectures not only will the time spent reading this book be doubly worth while, but we can be even more confident that future UK managers and leaders are displaying the required level of intellectual curiosity.

Given this proliferation of content providers, where should you start your search? An obvious source of guidance is the annual global MBA ranking, published by the *Financial Times*. The top ten schools in 2008, which would be an excellent place to start to search for relevant materials, were as follows:

- **UNIVERSITY OF PENNSYLVANIA, WHARTON —** www.wharton.upenn.edu
- **LONDON BUSINESS SCHOOL —** www.london.edu
- **COLUMBIA BUSINESS SCHOOL —** www4.gsb.columbia.edu
- **STANFORD UNIVERSITY —** www.gsb.stanford.edu
- **HARVARD BUSINESS SCHOOL —** www.hbs.edu
- **INSEAD —** www.insead.edu
- **MIT, SLOAN —** www.mitsloan.mit.edu
- **IE BUSINESS SCHOOL —** www.ie.edu
- **UNIVERSITY OF CHICAGO —** www.chicagogsb.edu
- **UNIVERSITY OF CAMBRIDGE, JUDGE —** www.jbs.cam.ac.uk

PROFESSIONAL ASSOCIATIONS, THINK TANKS AND CONSULTING FIRMS IN THE UK

A wide range of professional associations, think tanks and consulting firms are active in producing research reports and expert commentary on business and management issues.

In terms of professional bodies, useful material is provided by:

THE CHARTERED MANAGEMENT INSTITUTE – www.managers.org.uk

THE CHARTERED INSTITUTE OF PERSONNEL AND DEVELOPMENT – www.cipd.co.uk

THE CHARTERED INSTITUTE OF MARKETING – www.cim.co.uk

THE INSTITUTE OF CHARTERED ACCOUNTANTS IN ENGLAND AND WALES – www.icaew.com

Professional service firms in the United Kingdom, particularly the so-called 'Big Four' (PwC, Deloitte Touche Tohmatsu, Ernst & Young and KPMG), remain a useful additional resource for free public domain reports on key aspects of management and business practice. In addition to briefing papers on key industry sectors, they regularly survey CEOs and CFOs on their perspectives and priorities and produce research and reports on key management disciplines and challenges. They also provide a wide range of podcasts on topical issues.

Website addresses are:

PRICE WATERHOUSE COOPER – www.pwc.co.uk

DELOITTE TOUCHE TOHMATSU – www.deloitte.com/dtt/home

ERNST & YOUNG – www.ey.com/global/content.nsf/uk/home

KPMG – www.kpmg.co.uk

There are also numerous specialist business think tanks providing useful resources across the gamut of MBA issues. Useful institutions in the UK include:

THE INSTITUTE FOR FISCAL STUDIES – www.ifs.org.uk
NESTA – www.nesta.org.uk
THE NEW ECONOMIC FOUNDATION – www.neweconomics.org
SUSTAINABILITY – www.sustainability.com
THE WORK FOUNDATION – www.theworkfoundation.com

MISCELLANEOUS

MBA TV from LSE is available on youtube.com. MIT's Sloan School of Management has been releasing its lectures via its MIT World Service since 2001 (www.mitworld.mit/edu).

BIBLIOGRAPHY

Ahonen, T. T. and Moore, A. (2005) *Communities Dominate Brands: Business and Marketing Challenges for the 21st Century*, Futuretext

Anderson, C. (2006) *The Long Tail: How Endless Choice is Creating Unlimited Demand*, Random House Business Books

Barrow, P. and Epstein, L. (2007) *Bookkeeping for Dummies*, John Wiley & Sons

Bossidy, L. and Charan, R. (2002) *Execution: The Discipline of Getting Things Done*, Crown Business

Broughton, Philip Delves (2008) *What They Teach You at Harvard Business School: My Two Years Inside the Cauldron of Capitalism*, Penguin

Collins, J. and Porras, J. I. (2004) *Built to Last: Successful Habits of Visionary Companies*, Collins Business

Eastaway, R. and Wyndham, J. (2005) *Why do Buses Come in Threes?: The Hidden Mathematics of Everyday Life*, Portico Books

El-Erian, M. (2008) *When Markets Collide: Investment Strategies for the Age of Global Economic Change*, McGraw Hill

Fallon, P. and Senn, F. (2006) *Juicing the Orange: How to Turn Creativity Into a Powerful Business Advantage*, Harvard Business School Press

Friedman, Thomas L. (2008) *Hot, Flat and Crowded*, Farrar, Straus and Giroux

Friedman, Thomas L. (2006) *The World is Flat*, Farrar, Straus and Giroux

Godin, Seth (2007) *Meatball Sundae: How New Marketing is Transforming the Business World*, Piatkus Books

Godin, Seth (2006) *Small is the New Big*, Penguin Business Books

Goffe, R. and Jones, G. (2006) *Why Should Anyone be Led by You?*, Harvard Business School Press

Gore, Al (2006) *An Inconvenient Truth: The Planetary Emergency of Global Warning and What We Can Do About It*, Bloomsbury Publishing

Hand, J. and Lev, B. (eds) (2003) *Intangible Assets: Values, Measures and Risks*, Oxford University Press

Jaffe, Joseph (2007) *Join the Conversation: How to Engage Marketing-Weary Consumers with the Power of Community, Dialogue, and Partnership*, John Wiley & Sons

Jaffe, Joseph (2005) *Life After the 30-Second Spot: Energize Your Brand with a Bold Mix of Alternatives to Traditional Advertising*, John Wiley & Sons

Jenkins, H. (2008) *Convergence Culture: Where Old and New Media Collide*, New York University Press

Keough, Donald R. (2008) *The Ten Commandments for Business Failure*, Penguin Business

Kotler, Philip and Deller, Keven (2008) *Marketing Management*, 13th edition, Pearson Education

Leadbeater, C. (2008) *We-Think: Mass Innovation, Not Mass Production*, Profile Books

Lessig, Lawrence (2008) *Remix: Making Art and Commerce Thrive in the Hybrid Economy*, The Penguin Press

Lev, B. (2001) *Intangibles: Management, Measurement, and Reporting*, Brookings Institute

Locke, C. et al (2000) *The Cluetrain Manifesto: The End of Business as Usual*, Perseus Books

Lynas, Mark (2008) *Six Degrees: Our Future on a Hotter Planet*, Harper Perennial

McCarthy, E. J. (1981) *Basic Marketing: A Managerial Approach*, Richard D. Irwin

Mercer, David (1995) *Marketing*, 2nd edition, Wiley-Blackwell

Paulos, John Allen (1996) *A Mathematician Reads the Newspapers*, Anchor Books

Paulos, John Allen (2001) *Innumeracy: Mathematical Illiteracy and Its Consequences*, Hill and Wang

Penn, Mark J. (2007) *Micro Trends: Surprising Tales of the Way We Live Today*, Penguin

Pine II, J. (1992) *Mass Customization: The New Frontier in Business Competition*, Harvard Business School Press

Porter, Michael (2004) *Competitive Strategy: Techniques for Analyzing Industries and Competitors*, Free Press

Porter, Michael (2004) *Competitive Advantage*, Free Press

Raymond, Martin (2003) *The Tomorrow People: Future Consumers and How to Read Them Today*, FT Prentice Hall

Shiller, R. J. (2008) *The Subprime Solution: How Today's Global Financial Crisis Happened, and What to Do About It*, Princeton University Press

Shirky, Clay (2008) *Here Comes Everybody: The Power of Organizing Without Organizations*, Allen Lane

Spencer, L. Vaughan (2008) *Don't Be Needy Be Succeedy*, Profile Books

Stern, Nicholas (2007) *The Economics of Climate Change: The Stern Review*, Cambridge University Press

Tapscott, D. and Williams, A. D. (2006) *Wikinomics: How Mass Collaboration Changes Everything*, Atlantic Books

Wood, F. and Robinson, S. (2004) *Book-Keeping and Accounts*, FT Prentice Hall

Zeldin, T. (2000) *Conversation: How Talk Can Change Our Lives*, Hidden Spring

NOTES

INTRODUCTION

1   Broughton, Philip Delves (2008) *What They Teach You at Harvard Business School: My Two Years Inside the Cauldron of Capitalism*, Penguin

2   'MBA Students Swap Integrity for Plagiarism', *Financial Times*, 19 May 2008

3   'MBA Students Cheat the Most', *Financial Times*, 21 September 2006

4   See Shiller, R. J. (2008) *The Subprime Solution: How Today's Global Financial Crisis Happened, and What to Do About It*, Princeton University Press

SUSTAINABILITY

1   Stern, Nicholas (2007) *The Economics of Climate Change: The Stern Review*, Cambridge University Press

2   'Unquiet Ice Speaks Volumes on Global Warming', Robin Bell, *Scientific American*, February 2008

3   'Methane Bubbling Up From Undersea Permafrost?', Mason Inman, *National Geographic News*, 19 December 2008

4   Carbon Disclosure Project Report (2007), *Global FT500*, p.3

5   'Coca-Cola shifts Kerala bottling unit to Orissa', *India Times*, 22 March 2007, 'Killa Cola', the *Ecologist*, 1 April 2004

6   *Climate Changes Your Business* (2008), KPMG International

7   'Sustainability: Are Consumers Buying It?', PwC, 2008

8   Paulos, John Allen (1996) *A Mathematician Reads the Newspapers*, Anchor Books. Also see his equally wonderful *Innumeracy: Mathematical Illiteracy and Its Consequences* (2001), Hill & Wang

9   See 'Publication Probity', *New York Times*, 10 December 2006

LEADERSHIP

1   Richard Kovacevic in Pfeffer, Jeffrey (1998) *The Human Equation*, Harvard Business School Press

2   See Keith H. Hammond's 'Michael Porter's Big Ideas', *Fast Company* (2001). *Competitive Advantage* in particular remains a reference text for understanding competitive advantage, value chains and strategy formation.

    See also an excellent article by Donald Sull and Charles Spinosa (2007) 'Promise-Based Management: The Essence of Execution', Harvard Business Review, 1 April 2007. They explain how every company is, in essence, a dynamic network of promises made between employees and colleagues, customers, and other partners. They then outline in a highly accessible way how good execution is based on the art of making good promises inside an organisation. They believe good promises share five qualities – they are public, active, voluntary, explicit and mission based.

CULTURE

1   See the pioneering work of Baruch Lev, an accounting professor in the United States who has sought to establish new accounting principles to ensure that true value of intangible assets is more fully captured in the official accounts of publicly listed coporations.

2   Brinkley, I. (2006) *Defining the Knowledge Economy*, The Work Foundation

3   Corrado et al (2006) *Intangible Investment and Economic Growth*, Federal Reserve Bank Working Paper

4   'Trouble at the Office', *Business Week*, 25 August 2008

CASH

1   Davidson, S. (1994) *The Language of Business*, Thomas Horton & Daughters

2   Geijsbeek, J. B. (1914) *Ancient Double Entry Booking: Luca Pacioli's Treatise*

3   Woods, F. and Robinson, S. (2004) *Book-Keeping and Accounting*, FT Prentice Hall, p.26

4   Ibid., p.8

5   See CIPS, Knowledge Works – Knowledge Summary, Supply Chain Management (www.cips.org/documents/Supply_Chain_Management.pdf).

A popular test for undergraduate and MBA courses in Supply Chain Management/Logistics is Chopra, Sunil and Meindl, Peter (2008) *Supply Chain Management: International Edition*, third edition, Pearson Education.

See also *Harvard Business Review on Supply Chain Management*, September 2006, Harvard Business School Press.

CONVERSATION

1   This is part of a broader shift to on-demand viewing, which is also being driven by improved broadband speeds and the proliferation of viewing devices as customers use their iPhones and laptops to access recorded media. For example, the BBC's iPlayer is not the most visited television website in the UK, and had nearly 252 million requests for programmes in 2008. This is part of a wider trend that has seen traffic to video sites jump 48% in the past year ('Last rites for Christmas TV?', *Independent*, 23 December 2008).

2   Social software is the general term used to describe a plethora of new collaborative web tools, such as blogs, instant messaging and social network services.

3   See Tapscott, D. and Williams, A. D. (2006) *Wikinomics: How Mass Collaboration Changes Everything*, Atlantic Books

4   Thomas L. Friedman, in his recent book *The World is Flat*, identified the rise of what he calls the 'uploading revolution', in which a wide range of individually and community created information is made available via the internet, as one of his seven key forces 'flattening the world', and in his view the most disruptive of all of them. For Friedman, one of the most important aspects of this capacity to upload is that it is not merely isolated individuals putting their content on the web, but ad hoc communities which form and self-

organise to create and self-regulate the quality of the content.

5   Leadbeater, C. (2007) *We-Think: Mass Innovation, Not Mass Production*, Profile Books

6   Godin, Seth (2006) *Small is the New Big*, Penguin

7   See Jaffe, Joseph (2007) *Join the Conversation: How to Engage Marketing-Weary Consumers with the Power of Community, Dialogue, and Partnership*, John Wiley & Sons, p. 1

8   Godin, Seth (2007) *Meatball Sundae: How New Marketing Is Transforming the Business World*, Piatkus Books

9   Zeldin, T. (2000) *Conversation: How Talk Can Change Our Lives*, Hidden Spring

10 McCarthy, E. J. (1981) *Basic Marketing: A Managerial Approach*, Richard D. Irwin

11 Mercer, David (1995) *Marketing*, second edition, Wiley Blackwell, p.29

12 Ibid., p.30

13 For example, Booms and Bitner added another three Ps to the traditional Four Ps to make them more relevant for the service sector. Their 3 Ps were: *People* – people often are the service itself. *Process* – how the service is delivered to the consumer is frequently an important part of the service. *Physical evidence* – the context in which products and services are purchased, which is considered by some to be part of the product package. See Booms, B. H. and Bitner, M. J. (1981) *Marketing Strategies and Organization Structures for Service Firms*, Marketing of Services, Donnelly, J. and George, W. R. (eds), American Marketing Association.

14 See Jaffe, Joseph (2007) *Join the Conversation: How to Engage Marketing-Weary Consumers*

with the Power of Community, Dialogue, and Partnership, John Wiley & Sons, p.6.

15   See Jaffe, Joseph (2007), Tapscott and Williams (2006) and Leadbeater (2008) for this and other examples of community-led activism and ideation.

16   'Bank's U-turn on Student Charges' (http://news. bbc.co.uk/1/hi/education/6970570.stm)

17   Godin, Seth (2006) *Small is the New Big*, Penguin, p.185

18   'iGod: Could Apple Survive without Steve Jobs?' *Independent*, 18 December 2008

19   The term 'prosumer' was originally coined by the futurologist Alvin Toffler (see Toffler, A., 1980, *The Third Wave*, Pan Books), and has since been modified and used by other writers. Tapscott and Williams recently elaborated on the related phrase 'prosumption' (production/consumption) to refer to the process in which consumers are increasingly participating in the creation of products in an active and ongoing way (see Tapscott and Williams, 2006, *Wikinomics: How Mass Collaboration Changes Everything*, Atlantic Books, p.126)

20   For an extended discussion of the MINDSTORMS® robot, which this segment draws upon, see Tapscott and Williams (2006) *Wikinomics: How Mass Collaboration Changes Everything*, Atlantic Books, pp.130–31

21   McClure, Samuel M. et al (2004) 'Neural Correlates of Behavioural Preference for Culturally Familiar Drinks', Neuron 44(2), pp.379–387

22   For an early treatment of mass customisation, see Pine II, J. (1992) *Mass Customisation: The New Frontier in Business Competition*, Harvard Business School Press

23 'Johnson promises personalised NHS', www.guardian.co.uk/politics/2008/mar/02/health.labour

24 See Anderson, C. (2006) *The Long Tail: How Endless Choice is Creating Unlimited Demand*, Random House Business Books, p.5

25 Ian Morris, 'iPlayer Should be an Online Freeview' (www.cnet.co.uk)

26 See Bob Baker definition – on Chris Anderson's blog – The Long Tail (http://www.longtail.com/the_long_tail/2005/01/definitions_fin.html)

27 See Anderson, C. (2006) *The Long Tail: How Endless Choice is Creating Unlimited Demand*, Random House Business Books, pp.54–5

28 Ibid., p.50

29 'Personalisation, the Long Tail, and the Charge Against the Customer Monoculture' (www.socialcustomer.com)

30 Leadbeater, C. (2008) *We-Think: Mass Innovation, Not Mass Production*, Profile Books, p.100

31 Ibid., p.101

32 Jimmy Wales, the founder of Wikipedia, statement on Wikipedia (www.wikimediafoundation.org)

33 See www.wikimediafoundation.org

34 Ibid.

35 See Leadbeater p.15 for an excellent discussion of the dynamics of Wikipedia. For example, most of the editing is done by a relatively small group, and the project's success has come to depend heavily on a core of highly active participants who each look after a set of pages, eliminating vandalism and deciding on corrections.

36 Tapscott and Williams (2006) *Wikinomics: How Mass Collaboration Changes Everything*, Atlantic Books, p.71

37 iCrossing with Opinion Research Corporation (2007) *How America Searches: Online Retail*

38 See Paul Burani's Clicksharp Marketing blog – 'Wikipedia: A Marketing Channel As Powerful As It Is Free' (www.clicksharpmarketing.com/blog)

39 Godin, Seth (2007) *Meatball Sundae: How New Marketing Is Transforming the Business World*, Piatkus Books, p.77

40 Ibid., p.108

41 Locke, C. et al (2000) *The Cluetrain Manifesto: The End of Business as Usual*, Perseus Books

Also worth reading:

The classic marketing text is, of course, Philip Kotler's *Marketing Management*, with the 13th edition having been published in 2008, and it remains the most widely used text in graduate business schools. There are a raft of new marketing theorists worth reading. For example Seth Godin's work is incisive and fun, as is Joseph Jaffe's brilliant recent book, *Join the Conversation*. Locke et al's book *The Cluetrain Manifesto* is also an important backdrop to this chapter, which popularised the idea that markets are socially constructed – and should be thought of as conversations.

The segment on the Four Cs was also inspired by a number of contemporary accounts of personalisation and customisation. For example, the Lego Mindstorm Robot example is featured in *Wikinomics*, Tapscott and Williams' essential account of how they believe the rise of mass collaboration changes everything. Charles Leadbeater's recent book eloquently covers similar territory.

PICTURE CREDITS

We would like to thanks the following for kindly supplying material for use in this book:

BBC – p.18 (left)
Corbis – pp.57, 97
Getty Images – pp.18 (right), 35, 59, 61, 88, 118
Intergovernmental Panel on Climate Change (IPCC) – p.23
istock – pp.20, 26, 29, 63, 108, 114
LEGO® Group – p.116
PA Photos – p.80
Random House Business Books – pp.53, 54, 56
Wikipedia – p.124

LONDON BUSINESS FORUM

THE 80 MINUTE MBA LIVE!

80 Minute MBA live events are run exclusively through The London Business Forum. In these fun, high-impact sessions, Richard Reeves and John Knell bring the content of this book to life.

For more information or to book places go to www.londonbusinessforum.com, call 020 7600 4222, or email info@londonbusinessforum.com.

THE 80 MINUTE MBA WITHIN YOUR ORGANISATION

Is your company in need of some inspiration? If so, Richard and John can be booked to run *The 80 Minute MBA* event within your organisation.

To check their availability and costs call The London Business Forum on 020 7600 4222 or email info@londonbusinessforum.com.